What are the
about e-dat

"All of us have more love potential than we are manifesting. *E-dating Secrets* is the ultimate book to help you find it."

"No one knows more about the online dating industry and how to get the right results. I can always count on Stephany's credible advice for my radio and TV call-ins."

"Dating or not, every woman must read the secrets in this book! The question and red-flag section alone would have saved me from two failed marriages. I'm sharing it with all my girlfriends as the dating guide that could save the rest of your life."

"Everyone has fears about online security. *E-dating Secrets* goes beyond standard advice with background checking tips and e-security secrets most people wouldn't think of. Follow the advice in this book. You'll be more confident wooing when you know you're not being wooed for the wrong reasons."

"Oodles of fantastic e-dating tips, love the personal anecdotes! The '*Who are you and what do you really want*' section is invaluable for soul searching and soul-mate searching singles."

– Sharif Khan, Author, *Psychology of the Hero Soul*

"Finally, a book that includes the truth about both cyber-laws, and the spiritual laws of attraction. When it comes to attracting your perfect love match, *e-dating Secrets* is the most complete and delivers simple steps to consciously attract your perfect partner online."

– Jan Stringer & Stacey Hall, Co-authors,
Attracting Perfect Customers

"Sassy, knowledgeable, humorous, right on! Excellent advice whether you are starting out or whether you've been online dating awhile. *E-dating Secrets* is a personal journey of discovering yourself and putting what you want out there."

– Lynn Rose, Singer, Speaker, Radio/TV Host, Lynnrose.com

"I love this book because it's not just about how to find someone, but also knowing at heart who is the right someone and why, so you end up with a deep, lasting relationship."

– Chris Attwood, Co-author, *Staying In Love
When the Relationship Is Over*

e-dating

Secrets ™

e-dating Secrets™

How to Surf for Your Perfect Love Match on the Internet

STEPHANY A. CROWLEY

Cover design by Dieselcode Web & Print Graphics. Visit www.dieselcode.com
Interior design by Pneuma Books, LLC. Visit www.pneumabooks.com

Quantity Sales — Please email marketing@e-datingexperts.com. Special discounts available on quantity purchases of 25 or more books by corporations, associations and others who wish to use them as promotional giveaways or for re-sale.

US Trade/Bookstores/Wholesalers — Please contact:
marketing@e-datingexperts.com or call 1-877-837-4269

Media — Please visit the www.e-datingexperts.com/media. Journalistic reviewers may quote brief passages or excerpts for review purposes provided credit is given to Stephany-A. Crowley and electronic links are included to www.e-datingexperts.com. Final versions and article reprint rights must be provided to e-datingExperts.com for use in promotional publication to clients, members and affiliates.

Library and Archives Canada Cataloguing in Publication

Crowley, Stephany A
    E-dating Secrets : how to surf for your perfect love match on the internet / Stephany A. Crowley. — 1st ed.

ISBN 0-9734016-1-3

    1. Online dating. 2. Dating (Social customs)—Computer network resources. 3. Mate selection. I. Title.

HQ801.82.C76 2004   646.7'7'02854678   C2004-904627-6

Special gratitude goes to:

Kyra-Serene for her patience,
cooperation and sunny personality.

Ina and Michael for love,
understanding, time and space.

Bruce for lovingly embracing
and supporting my mission.

Eileen Moore for believing
and making this vision possible on the web.

Mark Victor Hansen for being an unwavering mentor
who saw something I couldn't see in myself.

CONTENTS

Secret #9 - See the Signs,
Use Your Intuition, Reject without Rejecting 161

Secret #10 - Use the Rule of Three...
Everything Good Happens in Threes 175

Foreword by Mark Victor Hansen

All of us have more love potential than we are manifesting. Everybody dreams of connecting with a soul mate who titillates and awakens their passion for life and love. At long last the world has an electronic way to fulfill that desire.

When done right, the ability to synchronize in time and space with your ideal other and taste test them in the safety and security of cyberspace makes seeking a soul mate effortless and elegant.

As an insider to the problem, Stephany created a model for herself that is a winning combination to inspire millions of others to find their ideal loving and lasting relationship.

It's likely all other vehicles to get to your ideal relationship have been tested and failed for you or you wouldn't be reading this book. Using the e-dating Secrets™ can get you to where you want to be with fearless confidence, finesse and panache.

Through Chicken Soup for the Soul, I've made a lifelong study of relationship stories. I know that everybody's story is merely a before picture, until they have found the love of their life.

Now with the tools, techniques, strategies and principles in this book you can create your ideal after picture.

You are embarking on the most exciting adventure of your life to fulfill your every relationship desire.

The e-dating Secrets reveal the path to finding near perfection in relationship.

Enjoy reading, absorbing and using my friend Stephany's brilliant insights.

Mark Victor Hansen
Mega Best-selling speaker and co-author of
Chicken Soup for the Soul and
One Minute Millionaire Series.

Reflections from the author

Anybody can get a date on the internet! However, finding the right person to date is far more challenging. It's all about purpose — your purpose for dating and your purpose in life. Consider this: You are extraordinary and you have an extraordinary life purpose to fulfill. Dating the wrong people, or worse, marrying the wrong person, can distract you or derail you from your right purpose and the things you are meant to do and accomplish in this life. If you've ever been divorced you already know that.

Whether your purpose for reading this book is the ideal fun date for the occasional Friday night or your one and only soul mate, you'll find expert advice on how to e-date safely and effectively and save yourself time, energy, money and potential heartache. As the title of this book suggests, we want to help you find your perfect love match, whatever that means to you.

More importantly, I want you to consider this an enlightening journey. If you follow the e-dating secrets in this book, you'll gain clarity for what you want, confidence in who you are and make better choices to get you what you want, need and deserve in relationships. My goal is to help you find that ideal person who you not only enjoy spending time with, but who is the one that lights you up and inspires you while you are passionately on purpose to fulfilling the life you were meant to live.

You've just taken a step that can lead you to living the life and love of your dreams. Although online dating has been around for a decade or so, you should consider yourself at the forefront. Online dating is evolving into a sophisticated art that can help you find the missing piece that turns your life into a masterpiece.

Can you really find the love of your life on the internet? That may depend on your definition of *love of your life*. For some, the love of their life can mean the most extraordinary, the most memorable or the most moving relationship, but not necessarily the most enduring. If you believe the claims of thousands who have found the love of their life or "soul mate" on the internet, then you know it's possible. Why not you?

Whether you've never tried online dating or dabbled in disaster, this book is meant to give you logical steps, practical advice, heart-hope and encouragement. There are a lot of online dating articles and advice out there. Most of it is outdated, simplistic or mediocre at best. At e-dating*Experts*.com™ we've not only lived through experience, but we're continually researching thousands of sites and stories so you can have all the best advice in one easy reference guide. We've been there, done that, and we will help you avoid mistakes and learn strategies that thousands have learned the hard way.

There's nothing more exhilarating than the daily thrill of knowing that someone is genuinely interested in you. At the very least, you'll connect with quality people, enjoy dating again. You may even make lifelong friends as I have. Of course, the vision I hold for you is to see you living exciting romantic adventures and finding the one that makes your soul sing on your way to fulfilling your destiny.

Find Love, Live Love, Give Love,

Stephany A. Crowley
(and the e-datingExperts.com Team)

I confess to being a hopeless romantic and eternal optimist; I have faith in destiny.

I believe that every heart wants, needs and deserves love.

I believe e-dating is the safest, most efficient and practical way for busy people like you to find the love you want, need and deserve.

I believe the e-dating Secrets™ will help you find and attract your perfect love match more quickly and easily than any other dating method.

I believe this process can help define you and the basis on which you choose to live.

I believe that at the end of this experience you'll be clearer, more confident and have a hopeful heart.

I believe that destiny, like love, can find you when you least expect it; the net just gives it a direction.

I believe life's too short not to live from the heart and put your heart on the line.

Most of all, I want to see you find e-love and hear your heart-melting story.

Stephany

e-dating

Secrets ™

In this chapter...

Welcome to the new conventional dating

ONLINE DATING: BETTER THAN BLIND DATES, BUSINESS OR BARS

When you're ready for love, you simply put it out there and love finds you. Right? I used to joke that when the time was right the Divine (the universe, God, or whatever you call it) would just deliver him to my doorstep. A few years, a lot of dates and two failed relationships later, the joke was on me. I was still seeking the love of my life, and the only person I saw when I rushed to the door was the FedEx man. What's worse, I couldn't get a quality date.

Everyone likes to think of the prom queen sitting at home on a Friday night crying in her soup. The truth is, she probably is. Why? Because the guys she wants to date don't ask! They figure she's already got a date with the local super-jock, or they won't risk rejection because they think she's out of their league.

There are plenty of attractive, single professional women who suffer from this thing I call "Cheerleader" syndrome. This is especially true if you're a single mom or happily divorced. Men often presume that the cute little kid at your side is apparent evidence of your happy marriage.

If you want to have quality dates, you have to meet quality people.
~ Stephany

So what's a girl to do? I was an entrepreneurial single mom working 16-hour days, running a business on the side and doing charity work a couple of nights a week as a board member for Habitat for Humanity. My friends were all happily married, and I had no time, energy or inclination for bars. Jeopardizing a business connection or mixing business with pleasure was a headache I didn't need. What about a blind date? Well, you love your friends, but they really don't know how to pick 'em for you.

As time passed, I figured if God was going to deliver the man of my dreams, my email box was a little more convenient than my doorstep. I answered an annoying little pop-up on my screen and started online dating.

In just over a year, my profile was introduced to over 17,000 men. Of course I didn't converse with or date all of them. But I did have the luxury of pre-qualifying those that were interested (and interesting) and selecting about a dozen to date in person. I don't say that to impress you, but to impress upon you the advantage of online dating.

Just think about that for a second. Even if you were to run around town and attend every business networking, social or charity function, how many prospects could you realistically meet in one night? How many could you get to know enough to decide if you'd like to date them? Can you see how the odds are much better online?

After learning the e-dating *Secrets*, my inbox was flooded with so many new responses per day my head would hurt. I've been wined, dined, flown across North America for dates and had some incredible romantic adventures. Finding dates in other cities when I was visiting on business was a matter of click and pick. This blew my mind! I already know that the same is possible for you.

Women always ask, "Where are all the romantic guys?" The answer is, they're online! What really sold me on online dating was the quality of men I met. OK, I've had my share of wimps, whiners and weirdo's. However, most were genuine, sincere, professional men who dared put their heart on the line, seriously interested in finding a woman with whom to share their life.

The majority of online daters say they are looking for a serious relationship, and yet somehow many of them are still dabbling in online dating two or three years later because they haven't yet found "the one." They look at online dating as a numbers game. It's not.

You can waste a lot of time and energy risking your heart with the *wrong* guy or girl. This book is much more than how to online date, it encourages you focus on *who* to online date. If you know you are ready and you take the time be clear about what you want, and be smart about how you go about it, it shouldn't take you years to find the love of your life.

Of course, they won't all be the ideal guy or girl long-term, but if you do it right, you're guaranteed to have some fun, daily e-mail thrills and a few romantic adventures for your memoirs.

HOW DOES E-DATING WORK?

No one ever said dating was easy; however, e-dating does make it simple. You start by surfing several recommended dating sites, pick one you like, create a *profile* (online résumé) and become a member. You will choose a catchy *username*, a nickname people can call you other than your real name. Then, click through a few multiple choice questions that describe yourself, your lifestyle, your background, and your ideal date or relationship. You'll write an essay blurb about who you are and what kind of relationship you envision, upload a few digital photos and post your profile on the website along with thousands or millions of other members.

Most sites will send potential matches that may interest you to your email box daily or weekly for you to view. You can search the site for potential matches based on specific criteria and characteristics and have dozens of potential matches instantly pop up to review.

When you find someone that interests you, simply send an email which goes through the site anonymously. Your profile is also sent to others who are looking for someone like you, and they can choose to contact you. If someone sends you an email, you can check out their profile before you decide to respond. After you've exchanged anonymous emails, getting to know one another, perhaps you decide to talk on the phone or meet in person. You either meet in person and live happily ever after, or you keep surfing until you find the one.

STATISTICS AND THE MULTI-BILLION DOLLAR INDUSTRY

Dating on the internet is growing exponentially! E-dating*Experts*.com estimated in 2003 that over 60 million (plus) singles world-wide are surfing to find their love match on the internet. This number is growing as online dating becomes what we call the "new conventional dating."

We believe that by the end of 2005, half of all the singles seeking relationships will be using the internet. Not only are people becoming more comfortable online, but more and more people login on their lunch hour from work, internet cafés, or libraries, even though they don't have a computer at home.

Although it seems like everybody knows somebody who has met someone online, there are very few credible statistics. Most dating sites boast their own statistics which are made up from surveys or polls of their own memberships and can vary widely from other sites. If you're looking to find out who the typical online dater is, chances are it varies from site to site, and calculation criteria really can't be compared. Many sites deliberately don't want you to know, because the truth is nothing to boast about. For instance, some sites boast millions of members but have a loose definition of membership and that may actually be spread over dozens of sites in a world-wide network while you're looking at a newer site with only a few thousand members.

Beware Before You Buy the Boasting

- Each site boasts different polling or membership numbers based on their subscriber base or whatever sounds attractive to their target market.

- *Membership* does not always mean active membership. It could include anyone who has ever been a member or yearly membership. Most sites let you post free profiles,

but you cannot send or receive emails until you subscribe. Many sites keep your profile (whether you come
back or not) to add to their list of faces. This makes a
"millions of members" claim much easier for them.

* "Subscribers" may be a more accurate term, but even
  then some sites include people whose subscription was
  only for a few months of that year and they may have ter-
  minated, hidden their profiles or gone inactive.

* Some sites rate themselves "Number One" because after
  their recent campaign they had over 50,000 new subscribers, while others judge themselves "Number One"
  because 86,000 new free profiles were created last week.

* Each site boasts varying and incomparable success rates.
  Some claim online dating success based on the number
  of email exchanges each day, others base their success
  on the number of matches they sent out. We found a few
  sites that boasted as high as 20% of their members found
  the love of their life, while others say they are responsible
  for over 50 marriages in the last two years.

* Few sites will reveal exactly how many men and women
  they have active or the ratio of men to women.

Singles Turning to the Net

In May 2003, e-dating*Experts*.com compared census data about
the number of single, married, divorced, widowed or separated
and compared them to the numbers boasted by the big sites. A
rough calculation estimated that the number of people actively

---

seeking love online was as high as 60 million world-wide. According to comScore Media Metrix, North America's preferred source for Internet Audience Measurement, *www.comscore.com*:

❀ In March 2004, the total number of unduplicated visitors to personals/dating sites (over the age of 18, all locations) in North America was 31.6 million.

❀ In the US, there were 27.0 million, 54% male (14.7 million), 46% women (12.3 million)

❀ In Canada, there were 4.6 million, 56% men (2.5 million) and 44% female (2.1 million)

Online Dating Statistics

❀ 22% of America's 98 million singles have tried online dating (American Demographics, February 2002)

❀ 56% of single Canadian adults connect to the internet weekly, compared to 44% of married Canadians and 26% of widowed, separated and divorced Canadians (Cybertrends, Fall 2000)

❀ 58% of all the individuals who use online dating services are looking for a long-term relationship, not to flirt online, find a marriage partner or find a sexual partner (MSN.ca February 2001)

❀ In North America, the dating services industry was estimated to be worth $1 billion (U.S.) in 1998 and projected to reach $1.5 billion by 2003 (Computer Industry Almanac)

ONLINE DATING IS NOT JUST FOR GEEKS!

In a survey done for MSN.ca in February 2001, of 1200 telephone and 6600 e-mail polled respondents it was revealed that there are two men for every woman among the more than one million Canadian online daters.

* About 85% of them are employed; about 55% of them earn more than $40,000 or more.

* More than 40% polled belong to clubs, and more than 50% attend social activities more than once a week.

* Over 83% of online daters have at least a college education, with 10% holding more than one university degree.

* Most (58% of men and 60% of women) were using online services to look for long term relationships.

This survey also stated that over three-quarters of people who had gone on a date with someone they had met online reported that they'd told their family, friends, and co-workers about how they had met their date.

Women Winning the E-dating Game

According to a two week survey of over 15,246 people (25% women and 75% men) posted online in February of 2004 at MSNBC.com and Elle.com it seems women are having the most luck.

- 58% of women and 55 % of men have logged on to a personal site.

- About 50% of women and 36 % of men said that personals sites have made a positive change in their social life.

- 44% of women e-daters and 33% of men say they're getting more dates, more sex, and more lasting love from online personals.

- More than 25% of women over 40 are finding a mate through online personals.

Industry Trends

There are literally thousands of new e-dating sites every week. Just like the communications industry, the online dating industry is experiencing significant convergence. Anyone can launch a dating site today. There are several competing dating networks which allow you to buy into their software shell and private label your own database of members. They do all the technical work and client service, and the buyer does the marketing. Thousands of sites are being added to the already-existing tens of thousands of online dating sites world wide.

It's a wild world where survival of the fittest means whoever can out-market, out-recruit members and out-deliver services, wins. Many of the undercapitalized start-ups of a decade ago who built their own home and created the online dating community are struggling to maintain membership with antiquated software, limited services and an outdated look. The next generation can simply buy a fancy new home, let someone else service it, and throw a party creating a whole new online community with multiple sites.

Some successful mid-level sites struggling to break into the big time with couple of million members are buying smaller sites still struggling to break through the million member threshold. The largest most popular sites like match.com are buying up the mid-level sites and creating strategic partnerships with internet and email providers like MSN and AOL.

TOP 10 E-DATING EXCUSES...
MYTH BUSTING AND TRUTH SERUM

1. *"It's too cheap, cheesy and unconventional."*
   Truth Serum: We live in a world in hyper-drive. The traditional dating models don't work anymore. E-dating is rapidly becoming the new conventional dating. We predict that within a couple of years more than half of all people seeking relationships will be doing so online.

2. *"Online dating is for liars, losers, lonely hearts and lusty old men."*
   Truth Serum: Stats prove it; the majority of online daters are professional, sincere, and educated with above-average earnings. They are social, romantic and looking for a serious relationship. For them online dating is the easiest, most practical, time-saving way to meet like-minded professionals. Ask around, chances are you already know someone who knows someone who has met their match online.

3. *"I am afraid to meet strangers online, it's not safe!"*

Truth Serum: (Hmm, meeting a stranger in a bar is?) E-dating is actually safer if you know the e-dating secrets. You can check someone out, stay anonymous, meet in a public neutral location and do a background check before they even know your name.

4. *"People lie and misrepresent themselves. You never know if they are who they say they are."*
   Truth Serum: Yes, and people lie in person too. If you know how to ask the right e-dating questions and do proper checks to verify information, your chances of uncovering deception are faster and easier online.

5. *"It's too impersonal; you can't really get to know somebody online."*
   Truth Serum: You can read between the lines of stories or poems and listen to songs that make you cry or laugh out loud. It's amazing how much you can feel of someone's heart and spirit in how they write. People often reveal much more online or on the phone with someone they've never met than they do face to face meeting for the first time.

6. *"I could never do that; I'd be too embarrassed if someone found out."*
   Truth Serum: Profiles are anonymous. Besides, if someone you know happened to stumble across your profile and see you online, why would you be embarrassed? After all, they are surfing too, and are probably even subscribed to the same site.

7. *"I'm social; I meet people all the time and have no trouble getting a date."*

Truth Serum: Ahh, yes, congratulations. So, why are you still single? Perhaps you're not meeting the right kind of people. You could narrow your search for the ideal match online and stop wasting time with the wrong person who just happens to be there.

8. *"The technology is too complicated. I'm not good with computers. I don't have one at home."*

Truth Serum: Dating sites make it easy. If you can send an email and click a button, you can e-date. More and more people who don't even have computers at home are logging on with anonymous accounts from the office on their lunch breaks and after hours at internet cafés and local libraries.

9. *"I don't have time to date."*

Truth Serum: This is the only dating method that you can do on your schedule rather than someone else's. You can do it in your spare time. Now wouldn't it be nice to spend your spare time enjoying fun, like-minded company with someone you know is compatible?

10. *"I'm not good at writing."*

Truth Serum: If you can speak, you can write well enough

to e-date. It's merely a conversation you type. Write the way you speak. Using a grammar or spell checker is easy.

WHAT ABOUT OTHER WAYS TO GET A DATE?

Traditional Ways

Blind Dates
Asking or allowing your friends or family to set you up can feel like begging for a date. You need to remember that meeting people is just as hard for them as it is for you, so what makes you think they'll have an easier time finding you the love of your life? You may end up taking your chances with a baggage-laden single loser because they feel sorry for him or her too. Not only will you have to deal with inquiring minds that want to know and give them updates on how it's going, but when it doesn't work out they'll feel insulted and ask "What was wrong with her?" or "I've known him for years; he's great!" Most of the time blind dates are a scary waste of time.

Business Connections/ Office
In the age of sexual harassment lawsuits, meeting someone around the water cooler should be completely out of the question unless you want to become the water cooler conversation. It's bad enough that when you're in sales and dealing with the opposite sex, people often presume you'll "discuss the deal over dinner." Why add the stress of secrecy to a relationship or jeopardize your working relationships or career if it goes sour? Besides, running into an ex everyday at the office can be painful. E-dating *Experts* insist mixing business with pleasure is never a good idea.

Bars

]If you think e-dating is intimidating, have you tried walking up to a stranger in a bar lately? This is the most inefficient way to meet the right person. You'll

Kissing someone you met at church can feel like kissing your brother.
~ Deidre Howard

invest too much time and money to get too few quality results. You'll sacrifice your beauty sleep to spend time getting ready, spend many late nights cruising the scene and engaging in mindless chit-chat, trying to get to know someone over the sea of voices, loud music and smoke. Not only does walking up to strangers take courage, you're not likely to go alone, so it takes courage for someone to walk up to you and have your friends witness their rejection. There's little to do but drink, wait, and hope that by the end of the night you end up with the phone number of the least offensive person you met. Worse yet, too many people wake-up with a stranger they thought looked much better after a few drinks, in low light conditions. If by chance you do get lucky and meet someone you'd like to get to know, you either have to give a stranger your phone number or leave with this stranger for a coffee shop date to decide if you want to go on a date! For women, willingness to leave with a man "to talk," often mistakenly signals sexual suggestion.

Church, Social Clubs or Associations

There's nothing wrong with this approach, but don't you already know everyone there? If not, people may clue in to the fact you were so desperate you joined just to get a date. You may have a lot in common, but not everyone is single. Fishing in the church pond is like dating in a fish bowl. You may feel pressure from parishioners in your congregation or discomfort if it doesn't work out and gossip can be painful. Besides, if you fail with one, the other prospects might form preconceived notions, have misconceptions, or be pre-warned and see you coming.

Singles Resorts/ Tours/ Cruises

These can be pricey and there are no guarantees and no escape once you are there. You could find yourself fishing in a small pond with the wrong kind of fish (i.e., not age appropriate). If you're already going on vacation, it might as well be someplace where you can have fun with single people rather than alone or as a third wheel. E-dating *Experts* does recommend these, but think about bringing a single friend so you have an escape hatch and can come up for air.

The Dating Service

Paying someone to set you up on a blind date is not only costly it is passé. You pay a premium for the promise that they'll prescreen a potential match and set you up on a minimum number of dates. Only their peacock parade is more like a shallow wading pool of people who are too lazy, too busy or too desperate to get a date any other way. You'll spend more time flipping through pictures and watching videos of date prospects than dating. There is an advantage to pre-screening candidates, but e-dating *Experts* can show you how to do that yourself in a couple of clicks and conversations.

Chance Meetings

Most of us know someone who bumped into their life partner by accident on the street or at the local Starbucks, convenience store or dry cleaners. Hoping that you are going to meet the right person by some random chance meeting is wishful thinking for most of us. Most professionals drive to work, drive home and spend their spare time cocooning at home. Many are too busy with careers, families and lifestyles to frequent public places consistently. Besides, too often bumping into someone on the street turns into a bump and run. It's a good idea for single people to get out there and meet people, but don't get your hopes up. Internet dating does provide significant advantage to people who consider themselves homebodies. You can cruise the scene 24/7 without even taking off your pyjamas.

e-dating Story
The stereotypical blind date disaster

My girlfriend sang his praises, so I decided to let her set me up. From the car, I watched men entering the restaurant to catch a glimpse first. Since I was looking for a 50-something professional, my heart sank when I saw the stereotypical blind date disaster walk in the door. He was older, had a bad toupee, wearing pants that were too short, a Hawaiian shirt and sandals with white socks. Somehow, I knew he was my date. I entered and we smiled through some reasonably benign conversation about why he never married. Then he started to make gurgling noises from the back of his throat, as if he was going to spit! Wondering if he was OK, I suggested he take a drink of water to clear his throat.

continued on p. 17...

Newspaper Personals

Too little space + too little information = One big waste of time and money.

E-dating *Experts* scratch their heads wondering why people even use them anymore. Many newspapers try to combine their personals with more modern services like internet listings and voicemail tele-personals to try to compete (and make extra money). Usually one ad will cost you as much as one month with a dating site and you'll pay a premium per minute to use the voicemail personals. You're still taking a random chance that your soul mate is going to read the newspaper on that specific day. Newspaper ads with premium services are outdated and will have you dating the dated, in other words, people that can't or won't join the internet age to use a computer. If you're going to be the internet savvy, progressive type, why spend more money to get less exposure when for the same effort you can get more exposure for less posting your "ad" on an internet dating site?

NEW Dating Services

Speed Dating

E-dating*Experts*.com recommends this newest form of dating because it is essentially high-speed dating for the real world. It's a less expensive version of the traditional dating service on steroids and a caffeine rush. You'll meet at a location and play musical chairs every few minutes to introduce yourself to eligible singles. At the end of the night you decide which individuals you'd like to see again and turn in a request form. The good services are social, fun, well-organized, convenient and let you see member profiles ahead of time. The bad ones are a competitive mix of multiple blind-dates under a time pressure. We like speed dating because you're likely to be grouped with age-appropriate prospects, they may do background checks and there's no

e-dating Story

...continued from p. 16

He continued to gurgle and hiss and made a gesture saying that what he really felt like doing was sticking his finger down his throat and... Needless to say, I lost my appetite, but endured the rest of dinner anxiously awaiting the check. When the check arrived, he grabbed it and began to murmur while adding up his "half" of the bill, conveniently forgetting to add in the extras and wine he ordered for himself. I offered to pay the whole check (it wasn't much) then he corrected his error, adding in the extras but forgetting to leave a gratuity, so I left it with my portion. I declined when he offered to have me follow him to his place not only because I was thoroughly turned off, but I was also afraid to see how this man lived. Obviously he was destined to stay a bachelor.

rejection on the spot. You'll only find out the next day if the person you are interested in is interested enough to see you again. On the other hand, this is ideal for sharp conversationalists who interview well, but shy people are at a disadvantage. Five to eight minutes is rarely enough to get to know someone, never mind compete for their attention.

Lunch Clubs/Dinner Mingles

Let's do lunch. It's quick, it's easy, and there's enough time to get acquainted. But it's still just another blind date. Hey, you're going to eat lunch anyway and e-dating *Experts* say this option beats eating alone. However, you're not just paying for lunch; you could be paying a premium for a lunch partner and in the long run spending more for fewer potential matches. Dinner clubs are a little different in that they are usually a fun social occasion with 8-10 single men and women sitting around the table. The dilemma arises when you're not sitting beside the one who interests you, when it becomes a competition or when you're too shy to speak up.

TOP 10 BENEFITS OF E-DATING

We asked e-daters what they thought were the Top 10 advantages to online dating. Here are some typical responses.

1. *Online dating saves time.*
   - "It's convenient. The internet is 24/7, I can answer in my own time."
   - "I can meet more people in less time. I'd rather spend two hours online connecting with a few people rather than two hours over dinner, getting to know just one at a time."

2. *Online dating saves energy.*
   - "It takes several dates before you get to know someone. It's easier to interact online than to run around town dating every night."
   - "Dating someone online is less stressful; you can even do it on a bad hair day in your pyjamas."

3. *Online dating saves money.*
   - "Meeting people online is much less expensive than going out to meet people."
   - "You can get to know someone before you spend money on dinner."

4. *Online dating helps avoid potential heartache, and lets you date by design rather than by default.*
   - "Online dating forces you to define the kind of person you want and need in life so you're less likely to settle for or get involved with the wrong person."
   - "Knowing your must-have's and deal-breakers upfront makes it quick and easy to spot them in someone's profile or email."

5. *Online dating is much safer than traditional dating.*
   - "You can stay fairly anonymous until you've had your questions answered and check them out."
   - "You can arrange to meet in a neutral public location, without giving out your phone number or business card."

6. *Online dating offers more opportunities to meet more people.*
   - "There are millions more fish in the internet sea than the local bar."

• "Sometimes you connect online with people that end up great friends."

7. *Online dating allows you to pre-screen, pre-qualify and predict your first date.*
   • "You can usually tell if your profiles match at a glance."
   • "You can get to know if you like somebody or have something in common before you agree to start dating. By the time you go out you are reasonably sure you'll have something to talk about and a good time."

8. *Online dating leaves you in control.*
   • "You decide what kind of relationship you're looking for and when to take it to the next level."
   • "You can stay on a first name basis, and you only have to reveal what you feel comfortable revealing."

9. *Online dating gives implied permission to ask and answer the tough questions up-front.*
   • "People are motivated to answer openly, if they want a date."
   • "It's easier to type a question when you're not looking into someone's eyes."
   • "When you're writing an email, you get to think before you answer."
   • "It's amazing what people are willing to reveal online anonymously that they'd never imagine revealing on a first date."

10. *Ending an online relationship is less complicated.*
   • "If you discover you're not an ideal match, goodbyes

are as easy as a Dear John email"

- "People can come on with life-long intentions and leave with the click of a mouse."

E-DATING EQUIPMENT

Contrary to popular belief, you don't need to buy a computer to start online dating. You can use any computer with a high-speed internet access. As long as you're diligent and consistent, you can e-date on your lunch hour at work, or login at a library, internet café, office supply store, hotel or even a friend's computer. If it's not your computer, be sure not to save any files or passwords so that others can't read your email. If you're using a computer at work be careful. Many companies now have spyware to monitor the appropriateness of your emails and internet activities. Web pages you visit may be automatically saved to a temporary folder and scanned using this software.

That being said, e-dating *Experts* recommend that if you're seriously looking for the love of your life, you will want to invest a few hundred dollars in a used computer and a printer. A computer doesn't have to be fancy or cost much, it just has to be fast enough to download web pages. As for printers, you're probably going to want to print your prospects' profiles and emails at some point. People often make the mistake of buying the newest combination or colour printer available for under $200. While those printers

Site Secrets

Do you know benefits we haven't thought of? Please tell us!

We're compiling the largest list of online dating benefits ever and want you to be a part of it.

Tell us your most fun, flippant or serious reasons to online date. E-mail info@e-datingexperts.com or go to *www.e-datingexperts.com* and click on the e-dating STORIES tab.

may be cheap, they are not meant to last and companies make more money on the ink cartridges, which will cost you about $25-$45 per month.

E-dating *Experts* recommend buying what we call "a good used beast." This means a reliable, high-volume, black and white laser printer that you can pick up at any used office/computer supply store for about the same price as a cheap new one. Just make sure it is made for many copies and has a big refillable or recyclable toner (ink) cartridge. We like the HP LaserJet models. These workhorses were built like tanks to keep reasonably and reliably rolling along.

e-dating Story

My confidence soared as I started dating again

Late last year, I'd reached my lowest point ever. In the space of one month, the father I adored was dying in hospital; I'd lost my job trying to care for him, and the love of my life decided he'd rather be with one of my best friends and forced the sale of my dream home. Any one of these was enough to drive anyone over the edge but suddenly I found myself very alone, without hope and without a home. For the first time I considered the unthinkable.

A friend tried for months to get me to start dating online, but my confidence was shattered. How could I ever trust anyone again? An e-dating Expert helped me write a profile and take some great photos, and I reluctantly put myself out there.

continued on p. 23...

Don't Date Dial-Up!

You will want to make sure you have a high-speed internet connection and service. Most dating sites are loaded with images and features that will have you waiting instead of dating if you have a dial-up connection. There are many inexpensive high-speed internet providers to choose from.

E-mail Accounts for E-dating

You will need a separate email account or web mail account

that you use only for online dating. This is in addition to your personal POP email account which you use for friends, family, business etc. Unlike a regular POP account, a web mail account is one that does not come directly into your computer inbox but goes to a private inbox on a separate website to which you login.

A webmail account is also more convenient because you can login to your email from anywhere you find a computer and an internet connection. Some dating sites include an email inbox on their site which is handy because you only have to login to one website. However, it's still better to have your

e-dating Story

...continued from p. 22
It's funny how you don't realize how much better love can be until you find something better.

Within days my inbox flooded with dozens of emails, compliments and romantic notes from quality eligible men who were really interested in me! My confidence soared as I started dating again. I was wined, dined and laughing again in the company of wonderful men several nights a week. I haven't found "him" yet but I love all this male attention, and the daily romance has given me hope. There's nothing more enlivening than a potential new relationship. I feel appreciated and beautiful and I'm having the time of my life. For all the other broken hearted, thirty-something women out there...e-dating, there's nothing like it!

own separate e-dating e-mail account so you can keep your email private and not monitored by the dating site. It's also likely that your e-dating prospects will ask for your private email account.

The easiest way is to get a free email account from a service provider like *www.yahoo.com* or *www.hotmail.com* that includes an updated virus checker. When you've filled out the registration forms, agree to the terms, sign in and look for the fine print that says, "Sign up for FREE E-mail (with a 2MB storage limit and without the other features)" and click on it to complete your free registration.

E-dating *Experts* recommend using a separate email account that you use only for online dating for the following reasons:

1. It's easier to remain anonymous until you want to be known.
2. It's safer than risking access or harassment through your personal email account.
3. It focuses your dating energy in one place rather than juggling multiple accounts.
4. It's easy to change. Eventually you'll get spammed out of your inbox with unsolicited advertising.
5. It's free so you won't mind closing or trashing it when you are done e-dating.

e-dating Story

E-move without a trace

I'm so glad I took your advice and created a separate email account for e-dating. To deal with the usual spam I set my account to auto junk mail, but there was a guy who was so unhappy receiving my "Dear John" letter he submitted my email to various porn sites. Another guy I dumped became the love-sick puppy who would never give up and sent me 10 emails per day! You never know who you'll run into, but it is nice to know you can pack up and e-move without a trace.

TOP 10 WAYS TO AVOID FRUSTRATION USING FREE EMAIL SERVICES

1. *Empty your inbox daily.*

   Once you've read and/or printed an email, send it to the trash. Most services don't count trash as storage, and you can set it to empty trash once per week.

2. *Get a virus checker.*

   You'll need your own virus checking software even if your

service provider has one. Never open an attachment without first running it through your own virus checker. McAffee or Norton are two leading brands.

3. *Register anonymously.*
   Some people choose to make up pet names and information to guard anonymity. Follow the registration process, select a username and password that you'll remember but does not contain personal information. I recommend not using names but labels or sayings that are memorable. For example: 4Whathappensnext@websitename.com, Just4U2Day@websitename.com, 2Lovemetender@websitename.com, Whisper4akiss@websitename.com, or 2flewover@websitename.com.

   Make up something fun that reflects your spirit or favourite things and will keep you anonymous to other e-daters. Keep Anonymous: Be aware that when you register with your full name, your name may be tagged in the "from" line to every email people receive even if you've chosen a pet name or alias.

4. *Avoid using your name, initials, birth date, etc.*
   Remember FREE webmail is not always secure to hackers or identity thieves. Never send personal information like addresses or telephone numbers.

5. *Guard your passwords.*
   Never click the "automatically save my password for next time" button. You may end up logging on automatically or letting someone else log on automatically. This is especially true when using public or office computers.

6. *Change your password weekly.*
   Use a password that is a combination of numbers and letters that you can remember and change. (NOT obvious personal information like birth date, age, address, area code etc.)

7. *Beware of file size.*
   Most free services don't offer a lot of storage space (usually 2-5 mgs), so you'll have difficulty receiving and sending large files (like multiple high resolution photos). To get around this we recommend that you try the following:
   - Remind people to send small files or ask them to send attachments individually.
   - Save large attachments to disk or a separate e-dating folder on your hard drive.
   - Print and save your emails in an accordion folder or use the e-dating *Secrets* Journal from e-dating*Experts*.com in a 3-ring binder.

8. *Use folders wisely.*
   Add a new folder to your inbox for each person with whom you engage in a series of conversations. This helps you store a history of emails without clogging your inbox. Some services empty your inbox of old messages automatically so moving them to folders may save them from a best before date.

9. *Save your draft emails as you write responses.*
   It's a BIG pain in the butt to write a brilliant response to someone and then have it blip off the screen, crash, or bounce you out of your inbox because you timed out. Going back and re-writing is not easy.

10. *Keep a copy in case you have to resend.*

Sometimes the person will not receive your email because their service provider thinks your email is spam or junk mail. It's a good idea to either compose the email elsewhere or send yourself a blind CC or BCC so you have a record of it that you can cut/paste and resend.

HOMEWORK: FIRST STEPS

❦ Start collecting a mini-photo album of 3-5 photos that reflects your multi-faceted personality, lifestyle and things you enjoy. There's really no excuse not to share a photo; most people won't respond without seeing one. Look for photos that are clear and recent and ensure that you are prominently featured.

❦ Take some new photos. Don't sweat it if you don't have a digital camera, borrow one from a friend for the weekend, or take photos on regular film and ask your photo shop to put them into .JPEG files on CD-Rom.

❦ Re-visit *www.e-datingexperts.com* and click the SITES tab to check out our most recommended sites, read unique features, and reviews and choose one. Although you don't have to subscribe immediately, most sites will allow you to post a free profile. We suggest you get one started even with basic information to help get a feel for what's out there.

In this chapter...

Know who you are and what you really want

Suddenly you realize you're one single person looking for a date. You're standing in a crowded room full of thousands of strangers. The crowd is a mix of men and women, gay and straight, tall and short, younger and older, of various backgrounds, looks, interests and intentions. What do you do? You could work the room questioning each of them if they are married or single, or even the right age. Or maybe you could chit-chat with each one to see if you have enough in common to know if it's someone you'd like to date. If you had the courage to walk up to a total stranger and start inquiring, how many of them even fit the basic criteria? How many could you connect with and how do you convey who you are before "the one" you are potentially looking for leaves the room? Online dating can be as hit or miss as the real dating world unless you know what you are looking for and how to narrow the field to find it.

The good news is, unlike this picture of the real dating world, e-dating lets you search through the crowd faster and with less risk of rejection. The bad news is, if you don't define the right person to fit into the picture of your life, you'll waste a lot of time surfing for them.

Two common reasons relationships and marriages break up is that neither partner knows themselves or what they really want and need in a relationship. Most of the time it becomes clear too late that they really were not that compatible in the first place. We've all heard people say:

"He wasn't the man I married."
"She wasn't who I thought she was."
"He really didn't know and accept me for who I was."
"She was always trying to change me."
"We stopped doing things together."
"We grew apart, wanted different things in life."

The most important step in finding the ideal love match is clearly defining who you are, what's most important to you, and the basis on which you choose to live. Some people think, "I just want to put myself out there and see what happens. Let fate take its course." Even fate needs a little direction! These people end up using one of the above excuses for ending a relationship. Yes, looking inside to understand who you are can be a difficult process, especially if you've never really done it. However, it's worth taking some time to be really clear before you begin dating. Clarity will give you the confidence to avoid wasting time with the wrong person.

Everyone has difficulty describing themselves. The clearer you are, the more easily you will craft an e-dating profile to attract the right person and be able to quickly recognize a person that fits. This will save you a lot of dating heartache by giving you a guideline so you don't get involved with the wrong person.

Why should you be embarrassed if people recognize you? After all, they're surfing the site too, aren't they? Once you've had a few thrilling email exchanges and your heart has pounded over someone special, you can stand proud and share

e-dating Story

Embarrassed? Who me?

My boss discretely mentioned one day that another colleague swore he saw my name on an internet site. Panic cringed my insides. I was shocked, embarrassed and unsure how to respond, since there's no shortage of rumour mills in our office. It took a few moments for the stun to wear off before I asked, "Really, who said that?" When he told me, the answer was clear. "That's impossible!" I blurted. "He couldn't have seen my name on a site, dating profiles are anonymous. It is possible he recognized a photo; I've had great luck attracting dates with my photos. But the real question is, what was he doing surfing dating sites on company time, isn't he still married?"

what a great time you're having. Don't be afraid to put the real you out there. In the end, people will be more interested in living vicariously through you than ridiculing you.

WHO AM I REALLY?

You are unique, and you have unique qualities and gifts to offer in relationship. When dating online, you don't have to be tall enough, smart enough, gorgeous enough or the most outgoing to feel good about yourself. It doesn't even matter if you have a few pounds to lose. It's about recognizing and feeling confident about your strengths. Dating on the internet is not about competing against others. It's about your attitude about yourself and holding your head high — not above others, just with others. There is no competition — only what and who is right for you. In fact, according to a February 2004 MSNBC.com/Elle.com poll, 79% of men and 72 % of women surveyed online said they would rather their mate have a high IQ than a perfect body.

You are a catch and you get to choose who is the right catch for you; who is worthy of catching your attention and winning your heart. You are who you are, you believe what you believe. Be yourself with confidence so you can be loved for who you are. After all, you want that special someone in your life to forgive you for your strengths and love you for your weaknesses, rather than merely loving you for your strengths and forgiving your weaknesses.

The way you see yourself may be very different from the way others see you. Everyone has an inner personality and an outer personality. So ask your close friends, "How would you describe me? What do you like most about me? What qualities do you see and appreciate most in me?" You may be surprised at the answers but use them to help paint a picture of you for that special someone. Now is a good time to open your e-dating *Secrets* Journal, reflect on the following questions. Don't think too much, just write whatever comes up. If you need help finding the right descriptive words you can refer to the list of qualities in the section of Secret #2 entitled, "Write Out a Top 25 List."

1. What three things do people notice first about me?
2. About what three qualities do people and friends often complement me?
3 How do my best friend, mother, and children (etc.) describe me to other people?

WHAT AM I ABOUT?

Decide now, what's really important to you? Whether it is sports, family, career or other, decide the basis on which you choose to live your life: values, beliefs, hobbies, friends, social/business circles, causes etc.

1. What are my main strengths, skills and talents?
2. How am I unique? What accomplishments am I most proud of?
3. What do I enjoy most in life, or about my lifestyle?
4. What three things in life do I value most?
5. What three things thrill me the most or bring a smile to my face?
6. What drives me or motivates me?
   (Is it money to buy toys, service to others, or recognition from my peers, etc?)
7. What kind of social life do I enjoy or not enjoy?
8. What do I do to take care of myself? What do I do that's just for me?
9. What do I like to do on my day off or just for fun?
10. If I had unlimited power to change one thing in this world for the better, what would it be?

EMPOWER YOUR FUTURE RELATIONSHIPS

How we behave in relationship is sometimes very different from how we behave with our friends or business associates. Each failed relationship can help us to grow and get clearer about what we would like, need, and absolutely can't stand in a relationship. It's helpful before we begin seeking our next relationship to reflect on the lessons of the past to help us get clear about our future. No matter how bad our previous relationship was, we have to reach the point where we are willing to own our role in it and our negative patterns before we can heal and get beyond them to the kind of relationship we choose to live. Empowerment begins with self-observation.

One of the most useful exercises I ever endured in order to heal from and forgive past relationships was very simple and only took about 30 minutes. It was based on the adage, "We often dislike in others what we most dislike in ourselves." This simple consideration made me take a hard look at myself, own my faults and forgive those of my previous partner. It was incredibly simple, empowering and very liberating, and I never forgot the lessons. I called it the blame game.

Taking an honest look at yourself is not easy, because it's often easier to be a victim of a circumstance and others. In the end holding on to a victim mentality hurts only ourselves and our chances at true happiness. A victim mentality gives us a convenient excuse not to change; we say things like:

"I can't help it; it's the way I was raised"
"I'm this way now because I've been burned too many times in past relationships."

However, it's only when we stop and dare to ask the truth of ourselves that we realize that we are in total control of ourselves in the next relationship. We discover that maybe the way we respond in relationship is a limiting pattern that doesn't get us what we really want in a relationship.

The truth is, you are never really a victim of your circumstance. You always have options and you always have a choice, you just haven't seen them yet. When you can clearly observe and accept your own patterns in relationship, you'll discover how you can empower yourself and make the shift necessary to attract the kind of relationship you want, need and deserve.

The instructions for the exercise are appended to the back of this book. It is at the back of the book because you should not read the instructions for this exercise until you are ready to go through the process step-by-step. It can result in a powerful emotional release and therefore you'll want to pick the appropriate time and place. It is very important to follow the exercise and complete each step without reading ahead to the next step, otherwise you will find it more difficult and less effective. One way to ensure you follow and complete each step in the process is to ask a trusted friend to read each step to you. If you are ready now, take out your e-dating *Secrets* Journal and a pen, sit in a quiet place and flip to the back of the book. If you are not ready now, make a note in your journal to do it at a specific time later today or tomorrow.

WHERE DID ALL THESE GARBAGE BAGS COME FROM?

You don't have to be Freud to know that we are influenced heavily by the relationships we witnessed growing up and our past relationships. Imagine carrying around huge garbage bags filled with relationship patterns, negative beliefs about love, attitudes and reactions we adopted along the way, reactionary habits. We all do it, everyday. It's emotional baggage. Sooner or later it gets heavy and burdens or smells up our relationships until we can no longer ignore it. How many times have we heard someone say:

"Why do I keep attracting the same type of guy?"
"Why does this always happen to me?
Women are all the same...."

"I thought he was so different from my ex,
but he turned out to be just like him!"

We tend to repeat the same patterns and attract the same type of person over and over. Some people call it bad karma, but I prefer to think of it as a mystery with a lesson that is yet unlearned.

I'm not a psychologist and you don't have to study the intricate complications of Freud's famous Oedipus complex to know it affects how we choose and relate to our partners. Psychologists will debate this ad nauseam for centuries to come. Simply put, Oedipus was a legendary Greek King of Thebes who was stubbornly blind to the truth about himself and unknowingly killed his biological father and ended up marrying Jocasta his biological mother. The theory comes from a line in the play where Jacosta remarks to her husband that many men have dreamed about sleeping with their mothers.

OK, maybe not literally, but if you think about it metaphorically it may make more sense. Have you heard sayings like:

"No matter how hard a wife tries, she'll never live up to
the memory of his mother."
"He's a mama's boy."
"No matter who she marries, she'll always
be daddy's little girl."
"Her heart belongs to daddy"
"If you want to know how a man treats his wife,
look at how he treats his mother."

For many of us, how we relate to and what we expect from our intimate partners parallels our relationship with the parent of the opposite sex. Our impressions and attitudes towards our parents are like filters through which we see and judge our intimate partners.

One of the most revealing red flag or stop-sign questions is, "Tell me about your mother?" or "How would you describe your father? Are you close?" The manner and tone in which someone answers this question can often give clues as to the way they'll treat you and the kind of relationship you may have.

When I discussed this topic during one of the e-dating University Tele-classes, a woman screeched, "Oh my God, You're making me realize why I date the men I date and where I go wrong." She went on to confess that her father was an abusive alcoholic and she had a very bad relationship with him. She said just thinking about how she would answer the question made her realize how she was giving the wrong impression to her online dates because she didn't know how to answer when they asked about her father.

You can bet someone else can spot it in seconds on the internet just by the way you express yourself and write your profile or e-mails to each other. Invest in the time to identify and toss out your emotional baggage before it sabotages potential relationships.

The difference between emotionally healthy and emotionally troubled people is that emotionally healthy people recognize baggage and old patterns as soon as they pop up. They decide to let them go and look for ways to grow beyond those patterns that do not work. The emotionally troubled never inspect the baggage long enough to recognize it as garbage and toss it out. They refuse to recognize their patterns or role in relationships and continue to dramatize and repeat old patterns until their relationships become strained and broken again.

A Big Concept with Simple Truths to Consider

- ❤ Chances are you will look for and be attracted to (good or bad) similar qualities of the parent of the opposite sex. (i.e., marry your mother or father)
- ❤ Chances are you will react to and treat your intimate partner, in similar ways that you do the parent of the opposite sex. (i.e., expect them to be like your mother or father)
- ❤ Chances are you will repeat patterns of relationship similar to ones you have with the parent of the opposite sex or the patterns of relationship that you observed in your parents. (Oh my, does this mean we become our mother or father? We all swear we won't!)

Please, don't start sending us letters about how your ex is different from your parent or how wrong I am. Just remember, I didn't make this up! It's only food for thought and it's worth considering if it will help you find the right partner and make better choices.

EMPOWER YOURSELF

1. How would I describe my parents' relationship?
2. What negative beliefs or attitudes about love, marriage or relationships have I observed or learned from childhood or by watching my parents?
3. What positive characteristics or relationship habits have I observed from my childhood or picked up by watching others?

4. What does relationship mean to me? What do I believe to be true about love? About marriage?
5. What kind of partner do I want to be in my next relationship?
6. What kind of extraordinary things do I want to create in my next relationship?
7. What could I do to become the kind of person that I'm looking to be with?
8. Who do I need to forgive in my past relationships to free myself and be ready and open for love?
9. What do I need to forgive in myself to be completely at peace with past relationships?
10. What do I choose to be that would magnetically attract the kind of person I'd love to be with?

EMPOWER YOUR LIFE

1. What do I need to do to create life balance, time and emotional space for a new relationship?
2. How do I love and nurture myself so I can show up in the new relationship whole and complete?
3. How can I create and feel love and support outside a relationship with friends and family so I can be less needy and give my best to my partner?
4. Who are three people in my life, with healthy relationships, who know me fairly well, that I can trust to support and give feedback, guidance, and advice in dealing with a new relationship?
5. What could I do to relax, let go and believe that I will meet the right person, in the right place at the right time?

BE EMPOWERED BY A PREVIOUS
RELATIONSHIP / MARRIAGE

1. What three things did I love and appreciate most about my former partner?
2. What did I like least or what drove me crazy?
3. What three things did I learn from my previous relationship?
4. What were my greatest strengths in the relationship?
5. What three things did I identify about myself that I need to work on?

EVERYBODY HAS A DREAM...WHAT'S YOUR DREAM?

Deep inside, we all have a dream. It includes the dream life, dream car, dream job, dream guy or girl and maybe even the dream dog. Most of us never really let it out because we are either afraid of what others will think, don't feel we are worthy, or feel it's impossible. You have a right to live your dream and ask for what you want. In fact, your thoughts create your reality. If you don't put your wishful dream into clear vision and clear intention in your mind, you can't make it happen. What you think about for your life and your relationships, you create.

Your life and what you want out of it is your choice. There is no right or wrong answer. When dating, it's perfectly OK to say, "This is not for me," or "This is not how I choose to live." However, it isn't OK to be wishy-washy and say, "I'm not sure," or "I could learn to live with that," and risk complication and relationship discord later.

This is your opportunity to change from dating by default to dating by design. You want to date someone who can understand, support and encourage you. Dating by default is settling for less than you deserve simply because someone is there and is nice, comfortable or convenient. You deserve the relationship of your dreams and it begins with you. You'll want to be clear about where you are headed so your ideal partner can know if they are going in the same direction. After all if you don't know what you want, how can you find the right person to share it with?

You can live the life you're living or you can choose the life you live.
~ Movie Quote, Chicago

1. What kind of career am I creating?
2. What are my top ten goals, visions or dreams?
3. What kind of lifestyle do I want to create? (Describe it)
4. Where would I like to be in 3 years? 5 years? 10 years?
5. If my life was perfect, what would it be like?
6. What would I like to change in my life?

WHAT IS THE RIGHT CHEMISTRY?

Nobody knows all the factors involved in falling in love. Is it the right chemistry, or is it a Divine and wonderful mystery? We do know that it isn't just common interests or similar likes, dislikes, background or values because many found themselves falling in love with people they had nothing in common with and we say that opposites attract. But that's more physics than chemistry, isn't it?

In chemistry, combining two elements produces a reaction by both elements, or creates a completely new substance. Perhaps it's the same thing in love and the exchange or reaction is the communication between two people. Most people would agree that if you can't feel love you can't fall in love, and the way we feel love depends on whether someone is communicating it in a way that we can understand.

To really fall in love with someone and feel loved by someone takes the right communication. It's common to see relationships where women complain, "I wish I had a man who communicated more," and men complain, "I can't figure her out, I don't know what she wants." We tend to communicate in ways that we understand, but we need to learn to communicate in ways the other person understands. Since we don't just communicate through words it's a good idea to figure out your own communication style so that you can identify the kind of person and communication you need to feel happy and fulfilled.

In other words, for you to have the right chemistry with someone, you both need to speak the same physical and emotional love language or be able to speak each other's love language. Your love language is made up of the ways in which you communicate or demonstrate love and the ways in which love should be communicated to you, in order for you to receive and feel loved.

There are two factors that are helpful to consider. The first is considering your love language, and second is considering how you process information and the style in which you best communicate your love language, either through words (auditory), through images (visual) or through sensation and physical touch (kinesthetic).

WHAT'S YOUR LOVE LANGUAGE?
WHAT WILL IT TAKE FOR YOU TO FALL IN LOVE?
Have you ever tried to communicate with someone from another country who didn't understand your language? Remember how uncomfortable it felt when they looked at you

with a blank stare? Remember the frustration?

The same kind of misunderstandings and discomfort can happen when a couple isn't speaking the same love language. It can lead to bigger frustration, arguments and resentment. Understanding the way you express love and receive love is key to understanding what it will take for you to feel happy and fulfilled in your next relationship.

Some say French is the language of love but in the book *The Five Love Languages — How to Express Heartfelt Commitment to Your Mate*, Gary Chapman, PH.D., a leading marriage counsellor, offers an in-depth study into the five ways we give and receive love:

1. Quality Time
2. Words of Affirmation
3. Gifts
4. Acts of Service
5. Physical Touch

HOW TO DEVELOP THE RIGHT CHEMISTRY ONLINE

The challenge some people have with online dating is that "it's too impersonal" and "you can't really connect with someone" or "get a feel for the real person." While it is true that initially you don't have the benefit of body language and seeing what someone is like physically, it is possible to intimately connect with someone online if you're communicating in a way they can understand.

Neuro-Linguistic Programming (NLP) suggests that although we have five senses (sight, hearing, smell, taste and touch), we process information in three ways: visually (seeing), auditory (hearing) and kinesthetically (touch, taste and smell). Each of us uses a little of all three, but we prefer, or dominate, in one way. How we process information determines how effectively we communicate in relationships.

This is why there is a growing trend in the online dating industry to make online dating a multi-sensory experience through audio and video clips.

Understanding the basics of NLP and language styles will help you to relate to, understand and communicate more effectively with others. Then you'll know why you seem to relate to some people more than others, identify and understand someone's communication to you, and translate your own communication into the language they understand.

"I see you talking but I can't hear what you're saying."
"I hear your words but I can't feel them."
"You're telling me something but I can't see
what you mean."

Kinesthetic Personality Clues

Kinesthetic people process everything bodily and checks to see if "it feels right." Internet communication can be a challenge because they cannot experience the other person physically. For them, nothing is completely real until they can touch it, feel it, or sense it in person. The heart pitter-patters for profiles and e-mails that use the language that touches them in some way, allowing them to get a feel for someone and sense the truth of what they are communicating.

In conversation a kinesthetic person uses language like: "My feeling is... it makes sense to me... hold on a minute... let me touch on another point... and my gut tells me." A kinesthetic person's dating style is to jump right in and try it, connect in person and figure it out as they go along. They will remember most what they wrote, how they felt and the activities you did together. You'll impress them with your gestures, caresses and kisses in a cozy atmosphere or a picnic of texture-rich foods in the park. The kinesthetic person's love language is most likely to be Physical Touch, Acts of Service and Quality Time that allows them to tacitly feel your love in action.

Visual Personality Clues
For highly visual people, "seeing is believing." They look for signs to see the truth revealed. They respond better to profiles with lots of photos and e-mails that use descriptive language that paints pictures, scenes or visual images in their mind. In conversation they use language like "Look at it this way... picture this... imagine that... the way I see it... and let me be clear." A visual person's dating style is to meet face-to-face, check each other out as soon as possible and see if it makes sense. You'll stand out in their mind by using creative and colourful language and sending pictures. The things you see on your date will be most memorable. They'll be most impressed by the visually stunning and active place you take them that stimulates their imagination like the latest action flick, museum, or art gallery. The visual person's Love language is most likely to be Gifts, Quality

Time and Acts of Service in which they can see full-colour proof of your love.

Auditory Personality Clues

The auditory communicator, on the other hand, wants to "hear it from the horse's mouth." They are always listening for something that sounds right and might not hear you unless you whisper in their ear. In conversation they use language like, "Listen, I think... sounds good to me... I'm in tune with that... let's talk it over." The auditory person's dating style is to pick up the phone and talk instead of writing letters. They'll remember what you said, the way you think, and the tone of your voice. You'll impress with your ability to listen, engaging in stimulating conversations at a dinner party, and the sweet nothings you whisper in their ear while listening to some pleasant music or the sound of rushing water. The auditory person's love language is likely to be Words of Affirmation, Quality Time and Acts of Service that get them thinking and talking about how much you love them.

In this chapter...

Don't date by default, date by design

Men are just as likely to date by default as women. Especially if the one they are dating makes heads turn. Dating by default is when you continue dating someone because the person is not perfect but nice, not compatible but convenient, not right but available right now. Deep down you know this person isn't the one you were looking for but you like them, you have fun together, and it sure beats sitting at home on a Friday night. You say things like:

"She's not perfect, but she is hot."
"He doesn't have all the qualities I was looking for but he's a nice guy."
"There's not a lot of chemistry but growing to love someone takes time. Right?"
"Maybe I've been too picky, I can't wait forever."

I have a friend who falls for guys faster and more easily than anyone I know. Every few months she goes gaga for the charmer who adores her perfect face and makes her laugh and is willing to wine and dine her. She says, "I know he's wrong for me" or "I know he's not the kind to commit but I'm just having fun. It feels good for now and who knows?" If she's home, she'll open the door whenever he calls. After months of dating the present guy instead of a guy with a future, she's attached, heart-broken and resolves to stop wasting time with the wrong guy and be available for the guy she really wants shows up. But when Mr. Right Now shows up again because he's got nothing better to do either, she goes with the flow instead of saying no. Is she shallow, immature or just desperately lonely and dating by default?

WHY SETTLE WHEN YOU CAN SURF?

E-dating makes it much easier to avoid the dating by default pitfall. At the same time, e-dating makes it easier to date dozens by default because they happen to be the one pursuing you. You know if you had seen their profile first, you probably wouldn't have responded, but since they're interested, you decide you should probably take a chance and see where it leads. To your surprise, you had a pretty good time and have something in common. After your third date he/she thinks everything is going great. Are you ready for another date? This is where too many people say, "Sure, why not?" Before you know it weeks have turned into months and you're in a committed relationship that you would not have chosen in the first place, but it's comfortable.

If you are faced with such a dilemma, there are two simple, soul searching, yes or no questions that can cut through it like a hot knife through butter. Simply ask yourself, "Can I see myself with this person long term?" and "Is he/she the one?" Don't let yourself cop out with "well, maybe." Just keep asking the same questions, trust your first response, and your intuition and it will become clear. If the answer is no to these questions, end it graciously, and move on.

The great question that has never been answered and which I have not yet been able to answer, despite my thirty years of research into the feminine soul, is "What does a woman want? What do women want, my God, what do they want? What does a woman want?"

~ Sigmund Freud, 1856-1939,
Austrian Neurologist,
father of Psychoanalysis.

MY MOTHER WAS WRONG... THE INTERNET PROVED IT

When I was about 12 years old, my mother, a typical older generation European Catholic, asked me what kind of man I dreamed of marrying. I prattled on with an endless list of all the qualities I would look for in an ideal man. Soon her chuckles grew into belly laughs. When she was done, this petite, gracious lady slowly raised one eyebrow, smirked and said, "Well, you know darling, someday you'll figure out that life and marriage is about compromise. You're too picky. That man you're describing doesn't exist. Don't you want to eventually have a family?"

I shot back, "If I have to compromise, then I don't want it. Besides, I don't need a man to be happy. I'll have a great career and I don't need a man to have a baby." At that she howled with laughter.

That affirmation became a self-fulfilling prophecy. Twenty years later I refused to marry the nice guys, failing at two long-term relationships where I thought, "just living together, free from the conventional bondage of marriage, is a good idea." By the time I figured out that the commitment of marriage wasn't such a bad idea, I was a single mom, over 30, struggling to get a quality date, and thinking, "Where are all the high-quality, romantic guys looking to get serious and settle down? Maybe Mom was right." As my faith in true love waned, I began to compromise. I dated whoever was available until I discovered all the high-quality, romantic guys... on the internet.

Could I really find a guy who had all the characteristics I was looking for? I was looking for a lot! The internet has everything else so why not? The first web site I went to had an endless questionnaire asking me for all the details about my ideal love. Quickly exhausting my 25-item list, I knew I was in the right place. Delighted, I charged ahead with keyboard and mouse in hand. Not only was I encouraged to be discriminating, I later discovered that the more discriminating I was, the less effort and time my search would take.

WHAT ARE YOU FISHING FOR?

There are millions of fish in the internet dating sea. Despite that, many people get frustrated, mostly because they are unclear about what they are looking for. Many people surf aimlessly, drowning in the sea of possibilities. Others catch the wrong fish, leaving a bad taste in their mouth and eventually dismiss every fish as rotten, while the good ones get away. Still others waste time trolling for a smorgasbord, which either flounder away or go bad while caught in the net. This only results in frustrated potential lovers or people giving up and getting hurt.

Decide now if you are looking for fun, friendship, companionship, relationship, life-partner, marriage, one-night stand, regular plaything or a walk on the wild side. Be clear. Be honest... with yourself and others. Say what you want up front. There are probably thousands of others looking for the same thing. You'll get it if you ask for it. If you don't ask, how will they know? Save yourself and others time, energy and heartache. If you meet someone online and you quickly realize that you are not a match, they'll appreciate and respect you because you helped to figure out the mismatch.

1. *What kind of relationship am I looking for?*
   Friendship; Casual dating (i.e. someone to go to movies with occasionally; dinner; company party or event); a walk on the wild side or casual sex; steady boyfriend/girlfriend; serious/long-term relationship; live together partner; marriage; family.

2. *In what time frame would I hope*
   to achieve that relationship?
   In a couple of weeks; 6 to 9 months; within a year or two; before a specific date, birthday, summer holiday, or Christmas.

3. *What would my dream date look like? What would we do?*
   Use imagination, the possibilities are endless: Biking along a river; botanical gardens; art gallery; jazz concert picnic in the park; Cirque de Soleil (live theatre); great golf; white water rafting/extreme adventure; sunset champagne balloon ride; a convertible at the drive in theatre; laughing at a comedy club; salsa dancing; piano bar or decadent desert club, etc.

4. *How often would I like to spend time together?*
   As much as possible/daily; once a week; several times per week; weekends only; a few times per month; practically live together; just someone to travel with occasionally.

> *Respect yourself, value your time, know your limits, and trust your gut.*
> ~ Stephany

5. *How do I feel about a long distance relationship?*
   Am I willing to move to be close to the one I love? How far? Under what circumstances, conditions? In what time frame? Any places I would not be willing to go (live)?

WHAT'S YOUR TYPE?

Beautiful souls come in all shapes, colours and backgrounds, but when defining the characteristics of your ideal love match, there's no such thing as being politically correct. This is the one place where having discriminating tastes is perfectly acceptable. How you choose to live and with whom, is your choice.

There are many characteristics to consider when defining an ideal love mate. What ethnicity, race, religion, and background is best suited to you? Perhaps you'll agree, this world could use a lot more co-operation, religious tolerance, and respect for other people's traditions.

Think about whether you could be happy living in an inter-racial marriage, multi-denominational family or cross-cultural partnership. It's OK to decide that these are uncomfortable for you, but it isn't OK to be wishy-washy up front, get with the wrong person, and get very complicated later on.

WRITE OUT A TOP 25 LIST

Make a list of the top 25 qualities you seek in an ideal love-match. Most of us have been through enough broken relationships to know what we *don't* want, but it is more valuable to know what we *do* want in a partner. The more specific you are, the easier it will be to read profiles and identify a

likely match. We recommend writing the Top 25 most important qualities in your e-dating Journal. If you need help, browse through the list below and rate each characteristic from 1-10 on a scale of importance and ignore the characteristics that are unimportant. It's also helpful to write specific preferences or notes of your ideal for each. This checklist will also help in the next chapter when crafting your online profile. It will provide the foundation for crafting a profile that is irresistible to the kind of person you want to attract.

Able to Ask for/Accept Help
Adaptable
Adventurous
Affluent (wealthy, successful, well-off)
Age Range
Ambition (Goals, vision, direction)
Articulate (eloquent, loquacious)
Assertive (Takes a stand, defends)
Athletic/Sporty
Attentive (To others/to detail)
Attractive (Physical traits)

Authoritative (In control, speaks with authority)
Balanced Lifestyle
Body Type (Vitta, pitta, kapha)
Children (Wants, has, doesn't want, living at home/away, grown)
Communication (Verbal, auditory, kinesthetic)
Cooperative
Conflict Resolution
Courageous (Risk taking, adventure, fearlessness)

Creative Minded/Artistic
Curious Nature (Interest in learning)
Diet (Meat/potatoes, balanced, vegetarian, vegan)
Education (Secondary, post secondary, graduate, doctorate)
Emotionally Expressive
Emotional Health (Past regrets, hurts, future fears)
Energy Level (Stamina, endurance)
Entrepreneurial
Faithfulness (Monogamous)
Family Life (Devotion)
Financial Habits (Scrimper, saver, spender, scrambler)
Financial Security/Stability
Free-spirited
Generosity (Time, energy, money)
Happy/Jovial Nature
Height Range
Honesty/Integrity
Horoscope Sign
Humility/Modesty
Humour (Dry, sarcastic, banter, off the wall)
Hygiene/Grooming Habits
Independent (Self-sufficient)
Industrious (Hard-working, diligent)
Intelligence
Interest in Parenting (Ability)
Interested in Others
Kind to Others
Leadership
Listening Skills
Loyalty (Friends, family, lovers)
Nocturnal or Morning Person
Nurturing/Loving
Organized/Neatness
Optimistic

Outdoorsy/Nature lover
Passionate
Patience
Personality (Outgoing, quiet)
Philanthropic (Charitable/ Volunteer)
Physical Chemistry
Physical Fitness (Regimen)
Playful
Punctuality
Race (Ethnic background)
Resilient
Respectful
Responsible (Home, children, cars, finance)
Romantic
Self-confidant
Self-directed (Self-reliant, decisive)
Sense of Style (Home/dress)
Sensitivity (Empathy with others)
Sensuality/Sex (Likes/dislikes/ frequency)
Shared Interests
Similar Political /Social views
Skills (Social, home, professional)
Sleep Habits (# of Hours, position, snoring)
Sociable (Social skills, grace, charm)
Solutions Oriented
Spiritual Practice/Tolerance
Sports Spectator
Strong Character
Supportive
Tactfulness/Diplomacy
Tolerant
Traditional (Roles/values/habits)
Unassuming
Values
Work ethic

After each date, review your checklist to see how they measure up and remind yourself before you get swept away and blinded by love (or lust) or too quickly dismiss the person.

WHO IS REALLY COMPATIBLE?
THE 5 FOUNDATIONS OF COMPATIBILITY

Some say there are three

things you should never talk about on a first date: Religion, Politics and Marriage. How ironic that those are three of the five foundations of compatibility in a relationship. Internet dating provides a unique opportunity and implied permission to explore these topics before you decide to have a date.

Religion/Spiritual

There is nothing more sacred than one's personal relationship with the divine, God, spirit and the universe. Spiritual beliefs or lack thereof rule people's attitudes, actions and lifestyles. It's important to consider if you are compatible in this area, especially since this is one relationship that is not likely to change and usually comes before any other.

Marriage/Family

If you are looking for something a little more enduring than a walk on the wild side or a one-night-stand, attitudes about marriage and family are fundamental. If one of you doesn't want marriage or family and the other does, don't waste each other's time trying to fit a square peg into a round hole. It isn't going to work no matter how much you are attracted to each other. You may date for a while, all lovey-dovey over each other, but one of you will eventually look for the exit sign.

Lifestyle/Social

There are also lifestyle considerations when seeking a life partner. If one wants to retreat to a cabin in the mountains and the other wants to be a talk-of-the-town socialite or travel cosmopolitan cities your wants and needs may become a tug of war. If one prefers to stay home, order in and read a book while the other prefers fine dining and dancing, you may have challenges. What common interests would your ideal partner have? Sports? Hobbies? What activities would your partner have to enjoy? In what kind of social circles and friends would your ideal partner be comfortable in?

Career/Financial

Most people spend most of their time working. There are many issues to consider regarding work, like time spent, distance, stress levels, type of work, safety, etc. Who would fit into your world and be able to support your choices? What direction would he/she have to be going in their career? Do you live to work, or work to live?

Reality Check

People don't change

If you feel strongly about something when you're not in a relationship, you'll feel even more strongly about when you are in a relationship. In the beginning we are punch-drunk with infatuation and tend to be more flexible. When that wears off, look out! Too many people compromise their values thinking:

- "He'll change." He won't.
- "She's not so bad." She is.
- "If I just love him more, he'll get better." He won't.

Most divorce lawyers will tell you that money is the number one argument that breaks couples apart. When the financial going gets tough, the not-so-tough get going... usually out the door. If you're not compatible in your attitudes and habits towards money, you won't see eye-to-eye. The endless negotiation will suck your relationship energy dry. Are you a scrimper, cutting corners where you can, regular saver, chronic spender, or do you scramble when there's too much month left at the end of the money? What attitudes must your ideal partner have toward finances?

Physical/Emotional Chemistry

Every relationship requires a certain level of physical compatibility and intimacy to thrive. When you think about your ideal partner, how are their grooming, personal maintenance, fitness, and hygiene? What about sexual chemistry, inhibitions? What communication styles and emotional availability does your ideal partner have?

KNOW YOUR LIMITS... DEFINE THE DEAL-BREAKERS

Deal-breakers are the things you cannot tolerate in a relationship. It can be big things like wanting kids, drinking/smoking too much, or spending money wisely. It may be as simple as "I can't see myself with a guy who doesn't dance." Or, "I won't date a woman who doesn't like sushi." Identify your deal breakers among the foundations of compatibility: financial habits, work ethic, religious beliefs, family, social habits, and lifestyle.

1. What are my must-have qualities for my ideal love match?
2. What are my would-like qualities for my ideal love match?

3. What are my can't-have qualities? (deal-breakers)

You're not likely to change, why should you? Who's to say that your attitudes and behaviours are any better (or worse) than theirs? You're just different. You'll want to decide if your differences complement or contradict each other. Decide on deal-breakers now to avoid tension and resentment later.

LONG DISTANCE LOVERS... LOVE KNOWS NO BOUNDARIES

My internet dates have asked me why I would be interested in someone on the other side of the continent. My answer: "Is it really realistic to think that your soul mate would be the boy next door?"

e-dating Story

Deal-breakers or simply guidelines?

For years I told myself, "I won't date computer techies or military men," or, "I won't date a man who is less than 10 years older than me," and "If he doesn't own a tux, or has tattoos, he's not for me!" I ended up falling for a guy who had just about every quality on my Top 25 List, plus he was former military, had three tattoos, worked in high-tech, and was only 5 years older! Obviously, what I thought were deal-breakers were just guidelines. My real deal-breakers were drinking or smoking to excess, wanting more children (I'm happy with my one angel) and tolerance of my spiritual faith. He taught me two unavoidable truths we must remember in matters of the heart. People are not always what they appear to be at first, and all things being equal, we really can't choose who we fall in love with.

There are a few things you want to decide before you embark on a long distance e-romance. Some people value love above all else; others value career, family, lifestyle. What's the chance of true love worth to you?

1. Distance can make the heart grow fonder. Less frequent contact means getting to really know each other, takes

longer... about 2 – 3 times
longer. In other words, if
exploring a new relation-
ship takes 3 months
count on at least 6 – 9
months to begin to get a

You can choose who you date, but you can't always choose who you fall in love with.

~ Stephany

real feel for each other. After all, it's not like you can run over for a cup of coffee and a quickie. Are you really willing to invest the time to explore a relationship?

2. Exploring a relationship online and by phone can only last so long without meeting face to face. We all lead busy lives and have many other priorities. Eventually life takes over. Are you willing to make the investment to fly to each other or meet in the middle? Are you willing to accept the possibility that someone else may enter the picture before you do?

3. Playful surprises in the mail, lusty email fantasies, sensual notes to each other and stimulating phone sex can be critical to keeping the relationship hot. When you meet in person the chemistry may not be the same as that generated by imagination. It's healthy to keep in mind before you visit that you're up for exploring the fun adventure and a great weekend, no matter what the outcome. Are you prepared to accept the possibility that the physical chemistry may not be there?

4. He turns out to be your dream date and it gets serious enough to consider long term — is there a structural fit? Exploring a long-distance relationship can be a significant investment in time, energy and money. Consider the

impact of hundreds in phone bills, airline tickets, travel expenses every month or two, and extra days off work, time away from children. Do you have the time and money freedom to continue this relationship and explore it more seriously?

5. You've fallen, this is it, and she's the one! The challenge of pulling two lives together in one place begins. Homes or furniture to sell, children to relocate, careers to alter. What's love worth to you? Is one of you willing to move to live the love of your life?

e-dating Story

Love at first email

When Robert first told me he was falling for a woman in New Zealand in a singles chat room in our spiritual community, I thought he was crazy. Even if they had their spirituality in common, how could it ever work? Their relationship thrilled daily and deepened online for months. When they finally met sparks flew, intuition and feelings were confirmed. She came to Canada to live together for a month. Before she left, they decided to marry and go through the immigration process. I was glad to be wrong when she became the most wonderful nanny my daughter could have had. Today both of them swear they knew they were soul mates from the very first email.

WHAT ABOUT ASTROLOGICAL COMPATIBILITY?

Have you noticed you happen to have friends with birthdays all around the same time? Have you noticed that there are certain people that you just can't get along with? Have you noticed that you are attracted to romantic partners with similar birthdays?

Whether you believe in astrology or not, it's just good fun to read about how the planets may be affecting you this week. After all, if there is scientific proof that the planetary alignment or lunar cycle can affect the tides and people's moods, then maybe an effect on your love life is not so far fetched. Personally, when it comes to love, I'd rather err on the side of believing because I can use all the help I can get. Besides, after a few years I started to wonder why when it comes to dating (and failed relationships) I seem to be a Capricorn and Leo magnet.

Many people regard astrology as a mix of superstition, paranormal and occult folklore because of the way it is presented and marketed by most sources as a mystic truth. However, traditional astrology is actually related more to astronomy. In man's early history it was based on and considered a science rather than a mystic practice. Astrological descriptions and forecasts were never meant to be carved in stone or tell fortunes. They were only meant to indicate tendencies and characteristic probabilities. From that point of view, it's logical to see why sages and scientists throughout the ages have witnessed striking consistencies of attraction whereby certain souls seek each other out and other combinations end up less harmonious. To astrology experts, what we call chemistry is simply two souls with compatible tendencies being irresistibly drawn to each other.

There are so many sources of astrology it's hard to know where to look and who to trust. Most will offer a mind-boggling array of complicated terms and combinations that will have so dizzy, you'll believe just about anything. So here are a few basics, just for fun, along with a little guide you can use when you begin dating to help know yourself and your potential soul mate.

In Western astrology there are 12 signs of the zodiac each with its own unique set of characteristics that have been linked to the position of the sun, moon and planets. The dates assigned to the signs often differ slightly to the actual dates of the con- stellations (alignment of the

Love knows no boundaries, so be open to long distance love. After all, do you really expect the love of your life to be the boy next door?
~ Stephany

stars). Most astrologers agree that most individuals can be assured of their astrological sign and tendencies. However, if you were born on one of the borderline dates, known as a *cusp*, (usually between the 19th and 23rd of the month) it's best to check the exact time and location (city latitude/longitude) of your birth. This is the only way that you can be sure of your sign.

The temperament of each of the signs is traditionally related to the fundamental qualities of Water, Earth, Air and Fire. In general you tend to get along best with people of the same temperament. Certain elements couple well together, Fire and Earth, Air and Water, the other combinations challenge each other. Here's an easy to remember example:

- ♥ *Fire* — (Aries, Leo, Sagittarius): Fire boils Water to steam, Fire burns Earth

- ♥ *Earth* — (Taurus, Virgo, Capricorn): Earth smothers Fire, Earth dams Water

- ♥ *Air* — (Gemini, Libra, Aquarius): Air feeds or is consumed by Fire

- ♥ *Water* — (Cancer, Scorpio, Pisces); Water puts out Fire, Water floods Earth

ASTROLOGICAL COMPATIBILITY SECRETS MADE EASY

In essence, all you need to remember about romantic compatibility is that "birds of a feather, flock together" and that the old adage "opposites attract" may also be true. In other words, similar characteristics will result in a comfortable relationship, while significant differences will create an interesting and more intense challenge. For instance someone born 3 months apart from you appears at a right angle (90 degrees) on the zodiac. This is likely your most incompatible love match as it may "square" you and be just different enough to end up on opposite sides of any circumstance. Although there is no such thing as an exact opposite, two people born 6 months apart may find very strong attraction because they are different enough to complete or balance each other. Sometimes they repel each other, but they often compliment each other and offer the best opportunity for personal growth.

Capricorn — December 22 to January 20

Determined; Disciplined; Patient; Steady

Constellation: December 14 to January 21

Ruling Planet: Saturn

Element: Earth

Most Compatible Match: Virgo, Taurus, Scorpio and Pisces.

Least Compatible Match: Libra, Aries, Leo, Aquarius, Gemini
Opposite: Cancer

Aquarius — January 21 to February 19
Friendly; Independent; Inventive; Original
Constellation: January 22 to February 14
Ruling Planet: Uranus
Element: Air
Most Compatible Match: Libra, Gemini, Sagittarius and Aries.
Least Compatible Match: Taurus, Scorpio, Capricorn, Cancer,
  Virgo
Opposite: Leo

Pisces — February 20 to March 20
Compassionate; Emotional; Romantic; Mystical
Constellation: February 15 to March 21
Ruling Planet: Neptune
Element: Water
Most Compatible Match: Scorpio, Cancer, Capricorn and Taurus.
Least Compatible Match: Aries, Sagittarius, Leo, Libra
Opposite: Virgo

Aries — March 21 to April 20
Courageous; Energetic; Impulsive; Optimistic
Constellation: March 21 to April 18
Ruling Planet: Mars
Most Compatible Match: Leo, Sagittarius, Gemini and Aquarius.
Least Compatible Match: Capricorn, Cancer, Scorpio, Pisces
Opposite: Libra

Taurus — April 21 to May 21

Affectionate; Dependable; Patient; Stable

Constellation: April 19 to May 10

Ruling Planet: Venus

Element: Earth

Most Compatible Match: Virgo, Capricorn, Cancer and Pisces.

Least Compatible Match: Leo, Aquarius, Sagittarius, Gemini, Libra

Opposite: Scorpio

Gemini — May 21 to June 21

Adaptable; Intellectual; Lively; Versatile

Constellation: May 11 to June 18

Ruling Planet: Mercury

Element: Air

Most Compatible Match: Libra, Aquarius, Aries and Leo.

Least Compatible Match: Virgo, Taurus, Scorpio, Capricorn, Cancer

Opposite: Sagittarius

Cancer — June 22 to July 22

Imaginative; Loyal; Receptive; Sensitive

Constellation: June 19 to July 21

Ruling Planet: Moon

Most Compatible Match: Scorpio, Pisces, Taurus and Virgo

Least Compatible Match: Libra, Leo, Sagittarius, Gemini, Aries

Opposite: Capricorn

Leo — July 23 to August 23

Creative; Exuberant; Generous; Powerful

Constellation: July 22 to August 10

Ruling Planet: Sun

Element: Fire

Most compatible Match:
Aries, Sagittarius, Gemini
and Libra

Least Compatible Match:
Scorpio, Taurus, Virgo,
Capricorn, Pisces, Cancer

Opposite: Aquarius

Virgo — August 23 to September 23

Analytical; Conscientious;
Modest; Practical

Constellation: August 11 to
September 17

Ruling Planet: Mercury

Element: Earth

Most Compatible Match: Taurus,
Capricorn, Cancer and
Scorpio.

Least Compatible Match:
Sagittarius, Gemini, Libra,
Leo, Aquarius, Aries

Opposite: Pisces

Libra — September 23 to October 23

Artistic; Charming; Diplomatic;
Easygoing

Constellation: September 18 to November 3

Ruling Planet: Venus

e-dating Story

A conversation written in the stars

I was e-dating a great guy on the other side of the country. We enjoyed sharing our histories and experiences by email and began talking on the phone. After awhile I grew tired of the casual "how was your day" phone conversation, after all we'd covered so much ground in email. So I asked him to tell me the exact time and place of his birth, of course he immediately guessed why. Neither of us really believed in astrology but just for fun I went to an online astrology site and produced a free compatibility report. The next conversation was so much fun. I read him the report and we laughed together. The report gave examples of strengths and weaknesses and raised a lot of questions. We found ourselves asking each other, "Have you ever done that?" and "Is that really you?" Suddenly, he couldn't help telling me personal stories as if playing a game of truth or dare. The section about how we would work together and even have sex together had us playfully cracking jokes.

continued on p. 69...

Element: Air

Most Compatible Match:
   Gemini, Aquarius, Leo
   and Sagittarius.

Least Compatible Match:
   Capricorn, Cancer, Pisces,
   Taurus, Virgo

Opposite: Aries

e-dating Story

...continued from p. 68

It was the best conversation we ever had! I really felt it gave us the opportunity to share deeper values and discover new things about each other that would have taken us years otherwise. We may have been miles apart, but we connected in the stars.

Scorpio — October 23 to November 22

Idealistic; Passionate; Persistent; Mysterious

Constellation: November 4 to November 16

Ruling Planet: Pluto

Element: Water

Most Compatible Match: Cancer, Pisces, Virgo and Capricorn

Least Compatible Match: Aquarius, Leo, Aries, Gemini

Opposite: Taurus

Sagittarius — November 23 to December 23

Clever; Explorer; Lucky; Philosophical

Constellation: November 17 to December 13

Ruling Planet: Jupiter

Element: Fire

Most Compatible Match: Leo, Aries, Libra and Aquarius

Least Compatible Match: Pisces, Virgo, Cancer, Taurus

Opposite: Gemini

E-dating *Experts* recommend getting a free online compatibility profile done, once you know each other well enough to ask for the persons date and time of birth. Since you're starting off as strangers, you may find it helps you identify and watch out for potential strengths and weaknesses between you more quickly.

HOW MUCH OF AN ANIMAL ARE YOU?

In Chinese astrology there are also 12 signs however they

are linked to the nature and character of certain animals. The story told in ancient scripts is that Lord Buddha himself realized that nations needed organization and called upon the animal kingdom to meet. Recognizing that people born in a particular year share certain common traits and qualities that animate their characters, he grouped the characteristics of the animals that showed up. This is why each year in a 12 year cycle is named after a different animal. To Westerners it may seem a little distasteful to be compared to a Pig, a Snake or a Rat, but the dominant traits embodied by these animals such as intelligence, cunning and social charm are revered and taken very seriously in the eyes of the Chinese. Similar to Western Astrology, the subtleties or nature of each character are also highlighted through five fundamental elements of Wood, Fire, Earth, Metal and Water. So what does your animal nature have to do with compatibility? Well, just think how compatible two tigers are in the same jungle or two roosters in the same house; as compared to two rabbits, two pigs or two rats in the same barn. It becomes pretty clear some animals just don't get along sharing the same space. Again, just like

Western astrology there's nothing meant to be carved in stone but it sure is fun to read about.

Site Secrets

Are you more or less compatible?

Visit *www.e-datingexperts.com/astrology* to find expert links to more free information about the characteristics of each animal and how compatible you are with individual signs.

Rat: 1912, 1924, 1936, 1948, 1960, 1972, 1984, 1996, 2008
Most Compatible Match: Dragon, Monkey
Least Compatible: Horses

Ox: 1913, 1925, 1937, 1949, 1961, 1973, 1985, 1997, 2009
Most Compatible Match: Snake, Cock
Least Compatible: Sheep

Tiger: 1914, 1926, 1938, 1950, 1962, 1974, 1986, 1998, 2010
Most Compatible Match: Horse, Dog
Least Compatible: Monkey

Rabbit: 1915, 1927, 1939, 1951, 1975, 1987, 1999, 2011
Most Compatible Match: Sheep, Boar
Least Compatible: Cock

Dragon: 1916, 1928, 1940, 1952, 1964, 1976, 1988, 2000
Most Compatible Match: Monkey, Rat
Least Compatible: Dog

Snake: 1917, 1929, 1941, 1953, 1965, 1977, 1989, 2001
Most Compatible Match: Cock, Ox
Least Compatible: Boar

Horse: 1918, 1930, 1942, 1954, 1966, 1978, 1990, 2002
Most Compatible Match: Tiger, Dog
Least Compatible: Rat

Sheep: 1919, 1931, 1943, 1955, 1967, 1979, 1991, 2003
Most Compatible Match: Boar, Rabbit
Least Compatible: Ox

Monkey: 1920, 1932, 1944, 1956, 1968, 1980, 1992, 2004
Most Compatible Match: Dragon, Rat
Least Compatible: Tiger

Rooster: 1921, 1933, 1945, 1957, 1969, 1981, 1993, 2005.
Most Compatible Match: Snake, Ox
Least Compatible: Rabbits

Dog: 1922, 1934, 1946, 1958, 1979, 1982, 1994, 2006.
Most Compatible Match: Horse, Tiger
Least Compatible: Dragons

Boar (Pig): 1923, 1935, 1947, 1959, 1971, 1983, 1995, 2007.
Most Compatible Match: Rabbit, Sheep
Least Compatible: Snake

In this chapter...

It's not love at first sight, it's love at the right site

WHAT'S THE BEST
ONLINE DATING SITE?

The best online dating site is the one that fits who you are. There are literally tens of thousands of sites out there, each with a distinct feel, target audience and mission. The good news is that there are more and more everyday, and if you don't get the results you are looking for from one site there are lots to choose from. The bad news is that there are more and more everyday and you need to examine each one closer and be more selective before you invest your time, energy and money.

There are basically three types of dating sites Popular, Specialty and Communities. Popular sites like match.com, date.com, yahoo.com and Americansingles.com cater to the general public of all ages, religions and backgrounds. They generally have millions more members, an extensive profile questionnaire and a database which is searchable based on very specific criteria.

Specialty sites cater to specific target markets: Either ethnicity, religion, socio-economic categories, location or age groups. They are very similar to the Popular Sites except their members all have something in common. For instance, there are sites for Jewish, Christian, Latter Day Saints, Muslims, Multi-faith, New Age and even Atheist singles. There are other sites in this category that cater to ethnicity like Asian, Black, Italian, German and interracial dating. Some are specific to teen dating, or the marriage-minded 30-something, and the over-40 first-wave baby boomers, or 50+ seniors. The dating sites specifically catering to less conventional relationships would also fall in this category such as swingers' sites, gay or lesbian, married women seeking flings and sites for couples seeking kinky sex, fetishes and sadism or masochism. Whether it's dating sites based on the type of pet you own, astrology or sites reserved for only the wealthy and beautiful, there's no end to the number of specialty dating sites available.

The third segment is a growing field of dating sites that offer communities which are usually based on the type of relationship people are looking for. The trend towards relationship communities allows you to post your profile on a website within another website which caters to people seeking friendship or companionship, romance or serious relationship, casual sex or intimate "adult" encounters.

As long as you are very clear about what you are looking for (Secret #1 and #2), it's a good idea to get your feet wet with a Top Ten popular site that has two to five million active members. This will ensure that you get results quickly, get a feel for the features and rapidly develop confidence in online dating.

E-dating *Experts* recommend that people post their profile on two sites. Once you have your feet wet, you may want to consider posting a second profile or switching to a specialty site to help refine your search.

THE TOP 5 THINGS TO CONSIDER WHEN SELECTING A DATING SITE

1. *Target Age Group, Ethnicity or Lifestyle* — Does the site cater to the demographic group you seek?
2. *Relationship Intentions* — Does the site cater to the kind of relationship you are seeking?
3. *Beliefs/Spiritual* — Does the site cater to or offer search options for your spiritual/religious beliefs?
4. *Location* — Do they have sufficient members in your area? Do you only want to date in your region?
5. *Features* — Do they offer enough convenient features for searching and safety?

e-dating Story

Anyone but this one!

When I first started online dating I joined a specialty site hoping to meet a nice Jewish man as a casual dating partner. I crafted a profile and diligently entered all the criteria I was looking for into the search engine. Imagine my chagrin when the one profile the site kept sending over and over was my ex-husband! I figured any site that would have him for a member was a bad sign. I moved on and finally met someone who's really compatible. Neither of us were looking to get married again, we live on opposite sides of the country and we're happy with our lives. We have a great relationship and meet at least 4 times per year to go traveling together.

WHY SURF FOR HOURS WHEN YOU CAN COMPARE IN A COUPLE OF CLICKS?

Visit *www.e-datingexperts.com* and click on the e-dating SITES tab to see our latest TOP TEN picks and get a feel for one that fits your character and style. Let e-dating*Experts*.com site reviewers surf for you, so you don't have to! Get all the facts, complete reviews and features list. Just pick the category, hold the CTRL key and click the links below.

- ♥ Find the best dating sites, with the best features.
- ♥ Easy to reference, compare sites with a couple of clicks.
- ♥ Read comprehensive reviews of unique features, see what the e-dating *Experts* think.
- ♥ Compare our feature tables, the most complete anywhere.
- ♥ Choose the site that looks and feels right for you.

• Top Ten Sites	• Free Sites
• Age Specific	• Single Parents
• Spiritual Sites	• Canadian Sites
• The Wild Side	• American Sites
• Ethnic Sites	• Dating Networks

Signing up is easy, just click GO! Click on the links or site banners to start creating your free profile or subscribe.

TOP 5 TIPS ON POSTING YOUR PROFILE

1. *Surf through a few sites first.*
   Each site has a unique look and feel, most will allow you to take a tour and see some profiles. Choose the site that matches your character, lifestyle and age group.

2. *Review other profiles before posting yours.*
   Draft your profile first so that you're sure it's a unique reflection of you. Then, review profiles of people like yourself, taking note of good and bad profiles, of both

men and women. This will help you to generate ideas and also make sure you're profile doesn't look like a copy of the others.

3. *Choose a fun and attractive username.*

   Your username is a nick-name people will respond to over and over again. It should not identify you personally but should reflect your personality. Make it a memorable reflection of who you are but never use identifiable personal information like a real name, age, birth date or address. For example: One e-dating woman we coached said her favourite perfume was Coco Chanel; she chose *Chanelkisses* as her profile username and email account. One e-dating man said his dog was his favourite thing, he chose *Blacklablover* as his username.

4. *Give each site at least three months.*

   Some sites offer a discount for commitment. A month can pass quickly and is not enough to give it an honest try. Commit to 3 months, and then decide if you'll move on. It can take up to three months to get used to a site, search through a large database of prospects and have your profile emailed out to potential matches.

5. *Avoid posting on more than three similar sites at the same time.*

   Some people are tempted to post on as many free sites as they

Reality Check

Three rules for selecting the right site

1. Big is not always better. (Neither is free; you usually get what you pay for.)
2. Fancier features do not mean better dates.
3. Finding the right site depends on what's most important to you.

can. Aside from the obvious time-consuming headache of juggling them all, it's possible some of the same people will notice you and you'll get a reputation for cruising or being desperate. This may stop people from responding to your ad.

TOP 10 TIPS FOR SELECTING THE RIGHT E-DATING SITE

1. *Search membership in your area.*

   Although most reputable

sites are globally minded, each one is based in a different city and naturally has more concentrated memberships in certain cities on the east or west coast. Look for sites that let you browse by state/province, city, number of miles from your postal code or telephone area code. Do a quick search for potential dates based on a few basic criteria (like age and location) and see how many members pop up. If it's less than 100, then think twice about subscribing. Search for another site which has more members in your region or select a regional site.

2. *Seek a look and feel that is you.*

   Does the site look and feel like your personality? Is it too flashy, too young, too professional, too dreamy? Posting on a site is a reflection of your character; make sure the site look and feel suits yours. Chances are, the kind of person you'd be looking for has a similar character too.

3. *Select your target market.*
   Some sites are specifically marketed toward a younger or wilder crowd, while others are targeted towards the professional, 30-40 marriage-minded, first-wave boomers, 50+, and ethnic or spiritual communities. Make sure the site promotion reflects the demographic target you are in, and are looking to connect with.

4. *Try free profile posting and browsing.*
   We recommend sites that let you enter as a guest, take a tour or offer a free trial period. It's better to browse before you buy or post a free profile. It can get annoying to have to post a profile on every site before you can even see what they offer. Smart sites have a member photo slide show to click through; maybe you'll find love at first sight.

5. *Use a two-way matching feature.*
   What if he's what you're looking for but you aren't what he's looking for? Trying to figure that out exchanging emails can be a waste of time. Smart sites offer a two way matching system which compares what both of you want and will only suggest or email potential dates that match both ways. Some sophisticated sites offer a "Do we match" button that compares your profiles at a glance.

6. *Create multiple photos or photo albums.*
   You have a multi-faceted personality and many looks.

Choose a site that lets you post 5 or more different photos. Some let you post up to 25 in a photo album. You'll want to see how people really look and show off the best you.

7. *Ensure sufficient space for a profile essay.*
You want to get a feel for people and give them a feel for you. Don't pick a site that limits the profile blurb to 100 or 200 words; pick a site that offers large space (1000 words) or unlimited and multiple opportunities to write about yourself.

8. *Choose monthly payment options.*
Dating is complicated enough without having to tax your brain to figure out if you have enough credits to respond or if someone's worth a response. Why pay per introduction when there are millions to choose from? By far the easiest solution is a monthly, no obligation, automatic payment in the range of $15-$35 with unlimited surfing and email exchanges. Plan to buy a 3-month premium membership to give the site an honest try at (at a slight discount), then decide if you want to cancel or just renew automatically. Be aware that your subscription may be automatically renewed, so remember to check out their cancellation procedures before you subscribe.

9. *Block members and check security features.*
People can be pesky, even after you've made it clear you're not interested. Choose a site that allows you to block emails from members or create a block list. Of course if you are sent something really offensive or out of control,

then you should report the member to your website security or administration.

10. *Make use of quick, easy searches and saved searches.*
Searching for your ideal guy or gal is fun. But if you're surfing a site everyday, entering all the search criteria over and over again is a bore. We recommend sites that let you select specific search criteria and save them with a search name so that you can search with one click the next day. Some sites let you save multiple searches with different criteria like Tall-Canadian-Blondes-25-35 or California-Professionals-with Children.

WHAT ABOUT CHAT ROOMS?

Most chat rooms are passé and nothing more than an online bar with the same thrills and dangers, sadly with the same results. For serious e-daters, chat rooms and Instant Messenger are two of the biggest wastes of time. There are stories of people who have encountered their soul mates in chat rooms; however, it's about as productive and efficient as trawling a net across the bottom of the ocean. You may find a lot of fish, but if you're looking for a particular one, you never know if you'll happen to drop your net in the right spot.

Chat rooms are like trying to have an intimate conversation with someone in a dark room, blindfolded while anyone can eavesdrop. Typically, chat rooms are set up like parties — anyone can enter, and hang out until they hear an interesting conversation. All the messages people send appear on the same screen, like a noisy party full of conversation. There can be anywhere from 5 to 35 people in a chat room at any given time, identified only by the catchy username they choose to login with. There's usually a small room list box to the right which reveals all the code names of people in the room. Some people have mundane conversations with each other, and others are just listening or lurking for the right opportunity.

Chat rooms were the original dating sites and were originally set up to provide a forum for communities of likeminded people to connect and discuss or debate specific topics. Chat rooms can be very useful to connect with people with common interests or in your area of expertise, study, work or hobby. They are also used to help members of clubs and associations to connect, ask questions and share information with each other. Beware! Some chat rooms can become very territorial.

While it is possible to meet some quality people, many public chat rooms are a haven for predators. It's where they find easy prey without introduction or accountability. There are countless stories of women and children seduced and lured for less than honourable intentions. Since chat rooms are the most anonymous way to connect, people can lie, deceive, change their names, change their stories and be anyone they want to be while they manipulate conversations. Some people do it just for kicks; others have more sinister motives.

The majority of people use chat rooms not because they

are seriously seeking love, but because they are bored or looking to avoid loneliness or just want to chat with someone to pass the time. Many chat rooms are a favourite hangout of pre-teen wannabe adults, over-the-hill adult wannabe teenagers, bored housewives and both male and female prostitutes luring people to escort services. You may find chat rooms specific to age groups and sexual orientation, rooms for gays, lesbians, seniors and single parents. But you should beware not to fall victim to pranksters, con artists and sexual thrill seekers.

e-dating Story
Adventurous but not that adventurous

I ventured into a romance chat room on a dating site and had a conversation with a couple of lovely women. We left the chat room and exchanged several emails. The first eventually confessed she was still a teenager (jailbait) and the other turned out to be a "mostly gay" man looking for a bi-sexual partner. What a huge waste of time!

E-dating *Experts* often hear women complain that when they meet men in chat rooms and go "private," it only takes about 5 minutes before the conversation turns to the sexual with a line like "What are you wearing?" or "Are you interested in getting it on?" We also hear men complaining that many chat rooms are populated with female escorts seeking guys desperate enough to pay for a date, or men posing as women on the chance that they'll snag a man willing to explore a same-sex liaison.

You don't need chat rooms to online date. Avoid wasting time and energy trying to get to know people there. You'll start at ground zero with little or no information and have to ask too many questions about basics like height, weight, location, marital status, etc. You can never be sure whom you'll meet, their real age, motivations or even their gender. The risk of disappointment and danger is too great.

One-on-One Chat Rooms

Some dating sites offer a one-on-one chat room that you can invite a date to enter for a private conversation. This is a form of no-frills instant messenger. E-dating *Experts* recommend that one-on-one chat rooms should only be used after you've reviewed each other's profiles, exchanged at least three emails each and are relatively satisfied that there is common ground and attraction.

We recommend that if you are subscribed to a dating site that offers the instant messenger feature that you turn it off or hide your online status every time you log on. If you don't turn your messenger off you may find yourself overwhelmed by several conversation requests at the same time that pop-up on your screen like spam in your inbox. Many people have a habit of surfing "who's online now" and wanting to talk with you because they're bored, desperate or just curious. This can be especially annoying when you are already in a conversation with someone and have two other conversation requests pop up at the same time from people who liked your photo and haven't even read your profile. Trying to have an instant conversation with someone you know nothing about can be very uncomfortable, frustrating and a bore. Typically, it goes something like this

e-dating man:	Hey, how are you today?
e-dating woman:	Fine, you?
e-dating man:	I noticed your photo and you're quite beautiful.
e-dating woman:	Thank you, I wish I could say the same about you
e-dating woman:	but haven't seen a photo yet.
e-dating man:	LOL, I was going to send you an email...

e-dating man: but when I saw you online, I thought I'd take a chance.

e-dating woman: So you're a guy who likes to take chances?

e-dating man: No, not really. Only with beautiful women.

e-dating man: So where do you live?

e-dating woman: Toronto. You?

e-dating man: Chicago. Have you been to Chicago?

e-dating woman: Nice city. I've been once.

e-dating man: I like it. How's your city? I've never been there.

e-dating woman: Busy, metropolitan but cleaner than NY. What do you do?

e-dating man: Do you have other favourite cities?

e-dating woman: San Francisco, Montreal, Paris. What do you do?

e-dating man: So do you like to travel?

e-dating woman: Love to travel. Didn't you notice that from my profile?

e-dating man: Oh, yeah, I see it now. I'm in sales. What do you do?

Bored yet? Once you've had this similar conversation with a dozen people, you realize it's a time waster that can be avoided by getting familiar with someone's profile first. You're conversations will have a better foundation and take on more stimulating depth.

IS IT LIVE OR IS IT MESSENGER? USE REAL-TIME CONVERSATIONS, AUDIO AND VIDEO

Instant Messenger is a real-time conversation where you talk with your fingers and get an instant response. This can be a

---

really fun way of getting to know someone and can also be an uncomfortably slow waste of time with someone you don't know. It's usually a free added service to dating sites or offered as a free service by companies like MSN, Yahoo.com, or ICQ. It takes a little getting used to typing and speaking in abbreviations and shorter sentences, but it's a fast-paced, exciting exchange and great comic relief for a few minutes a day.

Once you're interested in someone instant messenger is a great way to invite them to a live conversation without the long-distance phone bills. Most messenger systems let you exchange photos, and documents instantly. If you plug in a mini-headset with microphone to your computer, you can save your fingers and connect to a live voice conversation over the internet free!

Even if you're a neophyte or a technophobe, it's easier than you think! These are becoming very popular and you'll find each gadget is commonly available at any computer or office supply superstore for under $25. E-dating *Experts* consider these a wise investment that will truly enhance your online dating experience as well as save you money in the long run.

Better still, along with your headset and microphone you can inexpensively add a streaming video camera and see each other while you speak. This same equipment can be used to take advantage of the new trend in dating sites that let you record and upload a video clip to introduce yourself. E-dating *Experts* predicts it won't be long until all dating sites offer the streaming video feature.

Instant Messenger Etiquette

Instant Messenger programs provide some spontaneous and interesting conversations. However, just because someone is online, doesn't mean they are available and waiting to talk with you. They may be searching profiles, updating their profile, or chatting with someone else.

Beware that if your first move is an instant messenger "cold call," you're putting someone on the spot. It can feel as intrusive, presumptuous and offensive as a stranger ringing the doorbell to sell something while you're busy doing something else.

Make it a rule not to engage in an instant messenger conversation until you've first had a chance to read someone's profile and decide if you are really interested.

Never make a cold call, inviting someone to have a conversation without having first sent them an introductory email. This gives them a chance to view your profile and indicate their interest in talking with you.

Things to Remember When Using Messenger:

- Not everyone can respond all the time. Be patient, not peeved.
- If someone is typing a message, it's rude to interrupt the flow of conversation.

- In general, words in ALL CAPS ARE PERCEIVED AS YELLING.
- Save the name of your love interest in your buddy list and so it can alert you every time they are online.
- If you don't like someone, use the blocking feature so they can't request conversations.

- If you find yourself being ignored, the worst thing to do is to keep writing until the other person responds.
- Avoid sharing files through instant messenger.

In this chapter...

Write a WOW profile to irresistibly attract your perfect match

Your profile is not only your chance at a great first impression; it's a reflection of who you are. Everyone has difficulty at first writing their profile and describing themselves. It may not be easy, but it is simple. If you follow this simple formula you can't go wrong. Your goal is not only to turn heads, but also to share your headspace, tell them where your heart is, and get them headed in your direction. The good news is that you've already laid the foundation. This should be easier now since all the key elements can be found in your responses and notes from previous chapters. Refer to your e-dating *Secrets* Journal notes and your Top 25 List as a guide.

How irresistible you are starts with your *username* or *alias*. Make it short, sweet, memorable and easy to type. After all, it's the way people will remember you and refer to you over and over again. You'll need to think about this before you even register with a dating site to post a profile. You can use the same alias you used for your email account to make it more convenient for yourself and others.

It's amazing how many people still use their real names or bits of factual information that leave revealing clues. Other people make the mistake of using random letters and numbers that are too confusing to remember. Here are some examples to think about:

Poor Usernames	Good Usernames	Reason
John_Smith416	SnorkleBuddy	Reveal a memorable interest, not your name in a phone book.
2SEXY1961	CDNMapleLover	"Sweet" is always more attractive, proving you're sexy at any age.
Hot4U2Meet	TableWithView42	Make a date or make a wrong impression?
MJMcDonald	4MRGOLFPRO	A previous name like Mary Jane McDonald can be a new identity, for someone else! Try a previous activity instead (See Secret #8)
Bitzie1268	FunLovinSpirit	Itsy? Bitsy? Ditsy confusion of numbers no one can remember.

MEN SCAN, WOMEN READ

In general men and women read and respond to profiles differently. Although most men will only look at the photo and quickly scan what is written, you should take the time to put some creative thought into your profile essay and question answers. This is especially true for men writing to attract women because women will read the profile! Most women want to know that you can communicate and express yourself. If you leave blanks, click default questions or select "any" or "all" for your responses, people will think you are really not serious about finding someone.

The most important thing is that your profile is an accurate reflection of you. After all, they're eventually going to meet you and see the real you anyway. You'll want to be upfront, honest, descriptive and detailed, but you can also be playful and include teasers and challenges.

WRITE A PROFILE THAT WILL FLOOD YOUR INBOX

You're one in a million, literally. In a sea of millions of profiles you want to stand out and get noticed for what makes you unique. Sometimes, it's just one line that can irresistibly attract someone. Your goal is to get readers to blurt out, "That's me!" and, "I want that too." Don't worry too much at first about getting it perfect, just get it started. You'll be updating and refining it as you begin to see how people are responding.

Create an Intriguing Headline

Your headline is the deciding factor as to whether or not someone will read your profile. It's the first thing they'll read about you, and it's like a billboard ad that portrays an appealing image of you as a partner. It has to grab their attention in 8 words or less and make them click to know more. Make it unique. Headlines like "Looking for love" or "Are you my match?" or "Seeking Mr. Right" are boring and unimaginative. It's like saying "Nice guy" or "Ordinary girl next door." Come up with a compelling question or playful statement that expresses your unique style. Try highlighting your best feature, talent, attitude or hobby. Here are some examples:

- ♥ Long arms to embrace you
- ♥ Will you melt into my eyes?
- ♥ Do you have the slipper for my long narrow feet?
- ♥ Are you the pepper for my salt?
- ♥ Whispering lightly in your ear...
- ♥ I'll make you smile 'till your cheeks ache
- ♥ Laughing through life. Ready for a chuckle?
- ♥ If I promise I won't bite, will you nibble?
- ♥ Aim High, Value Love, Live your Destiny
- ♥ Zest for love, ready for life
- ♥ Inspired by passion
- ♥ Before you settle...click here
- ♥ You're only single once
- ♥ Water baby seeks man in wetsuit
- ♥ Sea and Ski with me
- ♥ I'm a bookworm...Do you have a Library?
- ♥ High flyer needs co-pilot to navigate sunsets
- ♥ I'm a detective, peak my curiosity
- ♥ Gourmet chef looking for the taste of his life
- ♥ Cute, Cuddly, and ready to create adventure
- ♥ I'm not the man my mother thinks I am, try me
- ♥ So much more than the girl next door

An Attention-Grabbing First Line

The first line of your profile is like a pick-up line that sets the tone and attitude of your profile image. Many times first lines are picked up by search engines on the dating site and will end up part of your billboard ad with your headline and photo. Use it to grab someone's attention. Try a line about your favourite thing, pastime, favourite quote or song, or your guiding philosophy. Make it a statement that gives a hint of who you are and makes them want to read more.

* Carpe Diem! Not only my guiding philosophy, but I hope that's why you clicked my profile.
* My life story? It pales in comparison to the life I can create with the right woman.
* Ball gown or construction boots, this chameleon is comfortable in both.
* I want to be the man my dog thinks I am.

A Fun-to-Read Profile Blurb (Essay)

Writing your profile essay is the opportunity for your personality to shine through to attract the right person. So have fun with it and make it an interesting read. In the spirit of fun, I prefer to refer to it in a more technical term - a blurb that makes someone "blurt"!

Start by thinking about your ideal match and what would be attractive to them. Keep in mind that you are not writing an ad to everyone, you are writing a letter specifically for the kind of person you want to attract. Go through your previous notes about who you are looking for and highlight key characteristics and phrases you can play with. After all, you have to use a certain kind of bait if you want to catch a certain kind of fish.

The best advice on how to write your blurb is to tell you what *not* to do. Avoid these 3 Common Rookie Mistakes:

1. *Avoid stating the obvious.*
Never use lines like "Hello there," or "Describing myself is

so hard" or "I never thought I'd be doing this." Don't waste space with a line that says how uncomfortable you are describing yourself. Everybody feels a little uncomfortable at first describing themselves, but to say so makes you sound insecure and less confident that what you've written is accurate.

2. *Avoid a negative first line.*
Don't open with a negative term, attitude or feeling like "Computers are so impersonal," "I hate meeting people in bars," or "Are there any good ones left?" These give the impression you're a pessimist and start the relationship on a downer. Instead make it positive and upbeat. People want to be inspired so use expressive descriptive words.

3. *Avoid the mundane.*
Try not to start your profile with "I am a..." or "My name is..." After you've surfed over a few dozen profiles they all

Reality Check
Keep it readable and real

• Don't use jargon - It's not a personals ad it's a profile... SWM, D&D Free, 40+ seeks SWF, 18-50 for sunset walks, just doesn't cut it.

• Use humour, but carefully – Your opening line may be cut off when posted. Be playful but brief, people may not understand the joke. I once saw a profile that read "Short, fat, bald, stupid seeks tall, thin, brilliant, blonde." It got shortened by the sites search window to "Short, fat, bald, stupid..." Ironically, that probably earned the man a lot of hits out of sheer curiosity.

• Keep it real - Avoid using dreamy idealism in your headlines. Phrases like "Prince charming seeks Princess" and "Fairy Tale in the making" may sound a little too unrealistic or fantasy-like to be taken seriously.

sound the same and melt together into one boring blur. Use something imaginative that will make you unforgettable and stand out.

An Irresistible Hook — A Playful Call to Action/Response

Just as the number one rule in sales is "don't forget to ask for the order," the most important rule of advertising is "include a call to action." In other words, tell them when, where and how to respond.

So they've read your perfectly crafted profile and they are interested. Believe it or not, they are less likely to respond unless you tell them to. You'll get more responses if you include a call to action at the bottom of your profile blurb. Try something like:

* Can't wait to hear from you...
* If that sounds like you, email me now...
* Let's explore possibilities...
* Let's connect...
* Could you be my baby? Send an email if the answer is maybe...
* Waiting to see your smile, send me your profile...

One of my favourite ways to induce a response is to include a trivia question, favourite quote or challenge. They will want to respond if they know the answer. I included movie quotes in my profile with a challenge to anyone who could name them. You can try any combination of playful trivia challenges that suit your passion for music, travel or philosophy. Here are a couple of examples:

* What happens when the handsome Prince climbs up the

tower and rescues the damsel in distress? She rescues him right back! (PS. I LOVE movies, extra points if you can mention the movie reference)

♥ All sorts of music can inspire me, but my favourite is the artist who sings "...a thousand rainy days since we first met..." on every CD. (Bonus points if you know who)

TOP 10 PROFILE WRITING TIPS

1. *Be Descriptive*
   Write more than 6 lines. There's nothing worse than clicking through to a profile to find out about something and finding nothing phrases with no substance. Too many people post a six-line profile with generic phrases like "down to earth," "fairly good looking," and "good sense of humour." You'll want to inspire people by giving something with which to identify. Avoid using terms that can apply to anyone. Describe your ideal love match, as well as yourself or the kind of relationship you long for. Think it through; don't be afraid to be specific and creative in expressing what makes you unique. You want someone to read it and

say "Hey, that's me!" and "That's what I want" rather than "Too bad they don't know what they're looking for" or "There's not enough to respond to."

2. *Be Conversational*

Write as if you are talking directly to someone. Use "I," "We," "You." Avoid using jargon. Don't use jargon like "SBF D&D Free Seeks SWM." This is a profile, not a personals ad. You don't want people to think you're lazy, empty or have nothing to say.

3. *Be Unique*

Avoid common phrases that appear in virtually every profile. Find different ways to express "walk on the beach," "candlelit dinners," or "love to travel." Avoid terms like, "Easy going, down to earth, fun loving." While these may be true, what does it really mean? You are much better off describing what you mean and giving an example.

- If you're easygoing you might say something like, "I go with the flow, when plans change, I change with it and enjoy whatever new adventure it brings."

- Down to earth can mean different things to different people. Are you a nature lover? Do you mean you adapt easily to new circumstances? Are you describing your outlook on life as well grounded or balanced? Is it that you like to keep things simple? Perhaps you mean you get along with all kinds of people?

- If you're fun loving, describe what's fun for you. "I'm a

social butterfly." "You'll find me on the dance floor." "I throw decadent dinner parties."

4. *Be Honest, Be Yourself*

Too many people try to be something they are not. Many people even lie about their weight, appearance, work or activities. Not everyone has to be the sexy, sporty, extreme adventure type to get a date. If you are bookish, introspective, like charity work or love foreign films, say so! Stretching the truth, exaggerating or misleading is a BIG waste of time and energy and will lead to a disappointing end for the both of you. Eventually the truth will be obvious and your date will feel deceived. You are completely unique, be proud of who you are and let that right somebody appreciate and love you for it.

e-dating Story
I wish it were really that way

When a friend posted a profile that said, "I enjoy running and training 3 times per week," I challenged her pointing out that she had not been running in months. Although she'd like to train 3 times a week, her work schedule rarely permitted it. I told her, "The last thing you want is for some super jock to meet you, eventually find out the truth and think you deliberately lied to impress him." I suggested perhaps it would be more accurate to say, "My work schedule keeps me busy but I like to run and I try to train 3 times per week."

5. *Be Creative*

Don't just state a fact, describe a feeling. Rather than saying, "I like great food and great wine," try describing your favourite food or restaurant. Paint a picture with words about how it feels. Be creative; have fun expressing your thoughts. You'll be creating something your prospect can relate to.

6. *Be Concise*

Don't tell your life story. Use short punchy sentences to create excitement rather than long drawn out explanations. You can still write a longer description if you keep the reader interested. While it is true, no one wants to read your life story, don't be afraid to write more and use the space provided. Most people will appreciate it and those that don't want to read too much will only read as far as they need to contact you.

7. *Be Modest*

Toot your horn, but don't be full of yourself. Avoid attitude, ego and bragging. You may be drop-dead gorgeous, drive a Porsche and have a sailboat, but you'll attract the wrong kind or give the wrong impression if you brag about it. Avoid phrases like "Everyone notices I'm extremely attractive," "I have a great body, like an underwear model," "I like my toys; maybe I'll take you for a spin with the top down in my convertible." Everyone should be proud of their accomplishments, but bragging is a bore. Modesty is the hallmark of people who are secure in themselves. Most people want to fall in love with a person, not a package. Stay real and don't make it all about you. You are much better off focusing your profile on the qualities of the person you are attracting.

8. *Be Safe*

Avoid giving out personal information. Never use your name, telephone number, age, city, or personal email. Don't give factual details like where you work, hang out, etc.

9. *Be Positive*

Leave the baggage in the closet. Avoid focusing on what you don't want rather than attracting what you do want. Never mention your ex or former girlfriends. "I don't want a woman who is shallow, dyes her hair or has breast implants." "Aggressive women and gold-diggers need not apply." "I don't want a guy who's so serious he can't laugh at himself or can't pass a mirror without combing his hair."...Can anyone guess what your ex is like?

10. *Be Accurate and Articulate*

Double check spelling and grammar. Don't shout — Avoid using ALL CAPS, it can feel like shouting. Review each statement to see if it is clear or can be misunderstood.

HOMEWORK: NEXT STEPS

♥ Think of a catchy title for your profile. This is the first impression to grab their attention! Think of a phrase that describes you, what you're looking for, your philosophy, your favourite phrase or song. Be playful; make it fun, light-hearted and positive. Avoid using negative words.

For example, "Sassy, Sensual and Seriously Seeking Soul-Mate" says more about you than "SWF still looking for nice guy."

❧ Create a digital photo album. Select 4-6 recent photos that express the many sides of you.

❧ Post your WOW of a profile that irresistibly attracts the right matches.

In this chapter...

Create a mini photo album to say a thousand words you can't

They say a picture is worth a thousand words. That's true, but a thousand responses to your profile are much better. People want to see who they are talking to. Posting a photo can get you up to ten times more responses.

DO I REALLY NEED A PHOTO?

There really is no excuse for not posting a recent photo with your profile. Perhaps you're lazy, not technically inclined or just don't want to be recognized. Dating sites are trending toward video, allowing up to 25 photos or search engines that let you search profiles with photos only. We predict the day is soon coming when you won't get a response without one. In fact, e-dating *Experts* don't recommend responding to anyone who refuses to post or send a photo.

The biggest mistake people make is posting old photos.

Worse yet, we've heard horror stories from both men and women who discovered their dates used faked, airbrushed or magazine photos. You want someone to fall in love with you for who you really are, not for who you used to be or wish you were. Even if you look in the mirror and think, "I haven't changed much," others will notice the grey hair, spare tire or crows' feet and feel betrayed.

Don't have a digital camera yet? No problem. Most sites will allow you to send in photos with a self-addressed stamped return envelope, and they'll scan them, post them and return them to you. We suggest borrowing a digital camera from a friend for the weekend. You can also take photos with a regular camera or throw away camera over a couple of days and then ask a photo shop to develop the film to .jpeg files on a CD-ROM or scan recent photos for you.

e-dating Story

Is that really you?

I met an intriguing woman online from another city who was both beautiful and intelligent. We exchanged photos and after a few email exchanges and telephone calls I drove for hours to meet her half way at a restaurant. When I arrived I couldn't even recognize her even though she was standing two feet in front of me. She was 15 years and more than a few pounds older. It wasn't that she was older that bothered me, it's just that starting a first date with deception is such a disappointment.

SHOW OFF THE MULTI-FACETED YOU...
PHOTO ALBUM GUIDELINES

Why not put up a mini photo album? Reflect the multi-faceted sides of your personality. Tell a story of different aspects of your life, hobbies, interests, how you live. Reveal the real you in a variety of looks and circumstances. Show off your glamour make-up in one photo and your natural side in another. Express your lifestyle out on the town, your favourite hangout, dressed for work, weekend casual, reading or even at a backyard barbecue or on a camping trip.

Whether it's your kids or cats, show people what puts a smile on your face. If you're a package deal and kids are important, include them in the photo and prepare your lovemate for the added dynamic.

Be mindful of the photo's you share. Although most people aren't going to misuse your photo or information, be sure there is nothing personally identifiable in the photo like a street sign, house number or licence plate.

Try posting a sensual romantic photo but not explicit or x-rated. You'll give the

e-dating Story

You look marvellous; photos keep the interest alive

My roommate and I both had 3-month, long distance online relationships. We were in desperate need of new photos to keep the fires burning. One evening we set up a backdrop, did our hair, make-up and nails and selected a wardrobe for a mini fashion show. We photographed each other around the house in different circumstances with different looks. We used a digital camera so we could edit, correct or crop the best shots. After two great bottles of wine, great music and laughs, we each had more than 20 photos each to keep on file for future use. In fact, it became a habit to carry a camera with us every time we went out the door together so we'd always have updated photos online.

wrong message and attract unwanted suitors. Remember, if you share a racy photo the temptation is greater to share it with friends. It may end up in other people's inboxes.

Take good photos specifically for use in your profile. Too many people use the cheesy photo from their best friend's wedding, or the half-ripped photo with someone's hand visibly draped over your shoulder or around your waist. Never use photos with the opposite sex, even if it's your sister or brother, it's a turn off. These give the wrong impression and tell potential love matches you're not serious.

YOU WERE BORN PHOTOGENIC! TOP 10 SECRETS FOR IRRESISTIBLE PHOTOS

How many times have you heard someone say, "I hate having photos taken," or "She's so photogenic!" The truth is, everyone was born photogenic... it's just sometimes the camera doesn't know it yet. Creating irresistible photos is easy in any circumstance. Memorize these ten secrets and you'll never have to shy away from the camera again. Soon people will be telling you, you were born photogenic!

1. *Shine in Natural Light*

   Most people look better in natural light. This is especially true if your face is sun-kissed. So take the photos outside with indirect sunlight or if inside use direct sunlight from a window. Your goal is to appear somewhat backlit, but be sure there are no shadows on your face. If you're naturally pale, choose less light or a lighter background.

2. *Use a Close Up*

   Photos taken from a distance with background images or landscapes take the focus away from you.

3. *Avoid the Loud Print or Hawaiian Shirt*
   Overly colourful or printed shirts take the focus off you. You'll look better in a darker solid color. You may look good in white, but it usually reflects too much in natural light or bright flash.

4. *Happiness Shows*
   Don't take photos unless you're happy. When you're feeling bummed or angry your eyes will always reveal your soul. Try excusing yourself for a moment to breathe, relax and compose your mind. Some people like to pray or meditate before taking the photos so their natural spirit can shine through.

5. *Pick Your Best Side*
   Cindy Crawford may be perfectly symmetrical, but you're not! It is true everyone has a better side. Experiment and ask a friend to decide. Never look square at the camera, instead try a shot looking slightly off camera. The shoulder of the person holding the camera can be a good target.

6. *Posture for Attitude*
   If an airplane adjusts its attitude in how it tilts, so can you. Turn your body slightly to one side, always drop your chin and your front shoulder slightly and tilt your head. You'll get a more dynamic, playful, take action look.

7. *Express Your Best Self*
   Play a little with your expressions. Practice your perfect Christy Brinkley smile (with or without teeth) in the mir-

ror until you can flash it without thinking. You can also experiment with the "pensive" look...Imagine you're asking a question to which you already know the answer.

8. *Chin Down, Look Up*
   Have someone take shots with the camera above your head... Use it dramatically by having someone stand on a chair, or use it slightly just to accentuate your features. Either way you'll look like you're having fun.

9. *Light on Dark, Dark on Light*
   Use a light background or soft backlighting, it is more attention getting online and you'll stand out. If your background is dark, make sure to wear a lighter colour.

10. *Watch Your Background*
    It's awful to have photos developed and discover there's a picture frame, flagpole or tree branch coming out of your head to make you look silly or draw eyes away from your face. Make sure your head is framed with space before you shoot.

In this chapter...

Flood your inbox and guarantee the right response

MAKING CONTACT:
MAKE THE BEST FIRST MOVE

Most people turn to the internet because they're tired of the bar scene. But not unlike the bar scene, the most important move you make when you spot a potential love interest is the first one, the pick-up line. Your opening line (or subject line) is the internet equivalent of making eye contact and smiling at someone.

You've already created an irresistible profile with an intriguing headline, an attention grabbing first line, and a fun to read essay describing yourself and your ideal match with an irresistible hook. But that only works if your perfect match happens to find your profile while they are surfing the net. What if you spot him or her first? You'll need to send them an email with a playful pick-up line that makes them want to click through to read your irresistible profile.

Like the cover letter of a résumé, it will determine if someone takes the time to read your profile or clicks the delete key.

You want to make an impression that sets you apart from the crowd and gets an enthusiastic reply. A clever opening line is the beginning of a great conversation that can last a lifetime. (Whew! No pressure!)

Once you've been online for a while, you'll discover that some people start a conversation with little more than a yawn like, "I read your profile, you sound nice," or "If you like my profile email me back." Sending an email like that will likely get little more than the delete key. Here are some examples of the worst opening lines...

- ♥ "Hi, my name is..." (You're not giving a speech are you?)
- ♥ "Hi, how are you?" (Too boring for someone you don't know yet.)
- ♥ "I read your profile and looked at your pictures." (Of course you did!)
- ♥ "I think we have a lot in common" (Really, like what?)
- ♥ "You sound interesting. I'd like to meet you." (Are you sure? Why?)

The cleverest responses I received were ones that caught my attention because they related to a line from a scene at the end of the movie Pretty Woman, which I included in my profile. Some of the responses included subject lines like...

- ♥ "I may not be Richard Gere, but you've got a Julia Roberts smile."
- ♥ "Julia has great teeth, but yours are superb! I'm a dentist and a sucker for a toothy smile."

🌸 "I'll take movies for $200, Alex"

The best way to get started is to find something in their profile that jumps out at you and get playful with it. It's not as difficult as it sounds to come up with a fun opening line that relates to a line in their profile. If there is nothing in the profile to respond to, you probably don't want to respond anyway. Here are some clever opening lines to give you an idea how to get started writing your first email to someone.

🌸 The gods must be smiling, because I sure am!
🌸 ... and there you were, the man I was searching for. I could tell by your profile you are...
🌸 The next time your dogs need a walk, perhaps we could walk them together?
🌸 Your children are adorable, I hope you find me that way, too.
🌸 So you like old movies? Well, as my friend Mae would say, "Hmmn, Why don'ch ya come up and see me sometime?"
🌸 Your profile screams perfection!
🌸 Blown away...You've been on my mind all day!
🌸 You made my day! I couldn't wait to get home to write you so I could tell you...
🌸 I'm a sushi lover like you, interested in sushi for 2?

If you don't have a lot of time to respond or aren't sure what to write in a letter, then you can take risk with a very clever one-liner to get somebody to read your profile, but there are no guarantees they won't just click <Delete>.

🌸 People are starting to notice the goofy perma-smile on my

face! I caught it from reading your profile. Do you have a cure?

♥ Can I pique your curiosity ...the way you've piqued mine?

♥ I'm WOWed...stunned... breathless...speechless...Help me out?

♥ Your profile made me smile, will mine return the favour?

WHO DESERVES A RESPONSE? EVERYONE

Remember every person who responds to your profile has put their heart on the line. They've responded to you because they saw something special in you and are genuinely interested. Keep in mind that they are as vulnerable to rejection as you are.

You don't have to respond to someone sending a wink or a smile" or a teaser, they are usually not expecting a response. People who send these kinds of winks and teasers are either too shy, too lazy, too cheap to subscribe or too busy trolling too many potential dates to send a real email. Sending winks and teasers is like winking at somebody across the bar to see if they take the bait. Usually there's not enough interest to buy someone a drink or get up out of your chair for a face-to-face introduction.

Similarly, I choose not to respond to men who simply attach their profile with no note, or who send a four-line generic form letter.

Of course whether you respond is your personal preference. However, I believe that if someone has taken the time to read my profile and send me a complimentary note expressing genuine interest, they at least deserve a few minutes to look at their profile and respond with a kind note. I don't want people to feel discouraged because responding to my profile was a waste of time.

e-dating Story

Charlie, your angels are not all the same. No form letters please!

One of my best friends was very excited to receive a response from a really cute guy who wrote a beautiful and very complimentary note. When she mentioned his username, I was sure I had seen it before and checked my notes. I discovered he had sent me the very same letter almost verbatim months before. Armed with that information she chose to seek someone with more honesty, sincerity and integrity.

WHY DIDN'T I GET A RESPONSE?

One of the most common complaints is that some people don't respond to emails. This leaves the sender not knowing if the message was sent, received, ignored or whether they should resend or send a different note and keep trying. The second most common complaint is people getting impatient, upset or sending rude messages when they don't get a timely response.

Stud or Dud?

If you don't get a response, it may be because you have run into a dud. A dud profile is one that is no longer active either because the person never sub-

If you don't think I'm worth writing to, why would I think you're worth dating?

~ Stephany

scribed to the service or they've found someone and moved on. Remember, most sites make you post a profile to let you have a look around or offer a free trial to help you get started. Unfortunately, some sites keep your profile up long after you are gone. They say it's just in case you ever come back, but it's really to add to the number of faces or boost the membership numbers they boast about.

Too Busy Juggling

Some people only check their messages every few days. We need to remember that people are busy and sometimes life takes over before you can respond to an inbox full of messages. The most common reason for lack of response is that most people try to juggle too many responses and lose track or lose interest. Either way you shouldn't take it personally.

While everyone who puts their heart on the line to contact you deserves a considerate response one way or another, that doesn't mean you have to get to know everyone or start a conversation with everyone. If you're clear about what you are looking for in an ideal partner, it's easy to figure out who doesn't fit the profile. Then it's simply a matter of being honest with yourself and others. Don't worry about potentially writing off "the one" or missed opportunities. If there is something in their profile that doesn't fit, or your first instinct is that they are not a match, it's not likely they'll ever be. Release them to find their perfect match and remember what you're looking for.

THE GUARANTEED RESPONSE FORMULA

The key to getting a response is to presume a friendly relationship and engage conversation immediately with the person as if you know them. It may seem bold, but it usually works because rather than asking for a conversation you are engaging one and they feel compelled to respond. Here is a simple formula to follow when approaching or responding to a love interest.

e-dating Story

Don't start something you aren't prepared to finish

When I started online dating I created a long list of the qualities I was looking for in a man. I thought, "Well, I have discriminating tastes and maybe I expect too much, but it only takes one." I was amazed and a little overwhelmed to discover that there were so many quality men out there that apparently fit the profile of what I was looking for.Excited, I started conversations with as many as I could juggle. Soon I was up until 3 am every night trying to respond to every potential match. So many emails, details and conversations I couldn't keep them all straight. Eventually I learned not to start something I couldn't finish.

1. *Compliment*

   Read their profile carefully to find something special in their attitude, photo or selected criteria to compliment them on. Make them feel as if you see who they are and honor their gesture. It doesn't have to be flowery, simply a kind word to help them feel good that they reached out and chose to respond to you. For example: "Your note captured my attention..." or "I noticed from your profile you are..."

2. *Comment*

   Look for something in their profile that intrigues you or that you have in common, then comment on it. Add your

personal point of view or
agreement with some-
thing they have written.
Try "One of my favourite
things is..." or "I particu-
larly liked..." or "I've always thought (felt, believed)..."

3. *Curious Query*

   Nothing is more flattering than letting someone know you
   are genuinely interested in what they have to say. Let
   them know you are curious to find out more about something you've seen in their profile beginning with " Have
   you ever noticed...?" or "What do you think of ...?"

4. *Compelling Question*

   Include a question or two at the bottom of your note. It's
   human nature to want to answer questions to which you
   know the answer. Even if they're not quite sure you are
   what they are looking for, they'll feel compelled to respond and you're more likely to get a note back. It's a
   door opener. See Secret #7 for Question ideas.

GETTING MORE HITS AND RESPONSES —
THE 7 SECRETS TO MAXIMIZE SITE SEARCH ENGINES

You're one in a million, but only if people find you. Online dating is a numbers game, the more people see you, the higher the
chances you'll find a quality date. Dating site search engines
are programmed to profile and rotate through millions of members to give them a chance to be seen. You'll want to make sure
you maximize the chances your profile pops up when people log

on, search or receive an email. Below are some of the secrets I used to maximize the search engines and get my profile introduced to over 17,000 men in one year.

There are ways you can maximize the search engine and ensure your one-in-a-million profile moves to the top of the list. If the search engine moves you to the top of the list, you'll increase exposure and the chances that your profile will pop up when people are looking.

1. *Post a Photo*

   Photo profiles get selected most often and some sites let you search profiles with photos only. Rotate or post new photos every couple of weeks, they'll send your profile out and flag you as "New."

2. *Update Often*

   Most search engines seek new or updated profiles to feature on their home pages, newsletters or search results. Submit your profile update every couple of days. Even if it's just to change your headline or edit a word or two, you'll be moved to the top of the priority list and give you a fresh posting as "Updated" or "Revised."

3. *Surf Often*

   Some sites presume that if you are online often, you are

actively seeking and will try to match you by sending your profile out more often.

4. *Be Online*
   Log onto the site as often as possible. Some sites have a "who's online now" option. Remember, dating sites want you to connect with other members as often as possible to feel encouraged, so when you're logged on you're a priority target for matching. Some e-daters choose to stay logged on to a site all day and minimize the site window while working.

5. *Pay the Price*
   Members who subscribe and pay in advance for several months or members who set up automatic payments sometimes get higher priority listings. Keep your account current.

6. *Spotlight Yourself*
   Every site has a member spotlight or profiles individual members from time to time in a newsletter or homepage. Make sure your profile set-up is set to submit your profile

Reality Check

The more specific you are, the more likely you are to find a match

Dating search engines depend on matching specifics. The more criteria you select, the more options they have of matching you. There is no such thing as being politically correct when defining the characteristics of your ideal date. This is the one place where having discriminating tastes is perfectly acceptable. It's okay if you choose to only date tall people, Republicans, and red-heads with tattoos or if you want to live in a beach house. Feel free to indicate that you dislike smokers, body piercing, vegetarians and if you don't want children, say so. The one exception to this rule is if the dating site has a small membership. In this case, if you select too few criteria or very specific criteria you'll likely get a "there are no matches for this criteria" message and you'll be encouraged to broaden your search.

for their member spotlight and auto-match or two-way match feature.

7. *Check Specific Criteria*

   Never choose "Any" or "All" when selecting criteria for your match. How can a dating site find your perfect match if "any" or "all" will do? Besides, your ideal date may think you don't know what you really want and pass you by. He or she is looking to see if "you have selected me!"

In this chapter...

Ask the right questions in the right way

They say love is blind, but maybe we just don't ask the right questions. When writing and responding to a date prospect, asking the right questions is the key to getting to know someone. Many people hesitate to ask questions because they are afraid of how they might look. We've been programmed by our society or parents with statements like:

"Their private life is none of your business."
"It's not polite to ask too many questions."
We shouldn't pry into other people's business."
They'll tell you when they're ready."

It's precisely because of these attitudes we learned that people don't generally feel comfortable raising certain topics or volunteering information. It is human nature to avoid discomfort and fear being misjudged or misunderstood. People won't tell you things unless you create a comfortable space to do so.

Not finding out about someone before you go on a date is like dating naked; you are raw, exposed and unprotected.

~ Stephany

It's amazing what people will reveal about themselves if you only ask the right question in the right way. How a person answers certain questions can reveal a lot about their character, their confidence, their readiness for a relationship and the challenges you might face.

Internet dating seems to give people implied permission to ask anything up front. After all, if they want a date with you and they are interested, they'll feel compelled to answer. The somewhat impersonal feel of responding to a computer screen often makes people feel more comfortable asking questions they would never dare ask on a conventional first date. What's more, people will often reveal beautifully written, well thought out answers to very personal questions with honesty and integrity when in other circumstances, they might think "that's none of your business." It's easier to get detailed information when they are long distance, as they'll feel safer because of the distance.

I'm inquisitive by nature and like to really get to know people. Most of the time, if done right people are flattered that you are genuinely interested in them or how they feel about things. Sometimes people are impressed and respect the fact that you had the courage to ask. In some cases, I've had my dates say, "I'm so glad you asked. I wasn't sure how to bring it up. I feel better now that it's in the open. Thanks for taking that monkey off my back."

HOW TO BECOME A MEMORABLE CONVERSATIONALIST

Carry a Conversation in Four Words or Less

People love to talk about themselves and be heard. The best way to build rapport is to listen, ask questions and let them talk. After all, isn't the goal of a first meeting to find out as much as you can about the other person? Getting deep into a conversation and keeping it going is simple. Whenever he/she tells you something simply ask one of the four following open ended questions:

* Really, why?
* Really, how?
* Really, like what?
* Really, tell me more?

Ask about What's Important to You

You should base your questions on what you value most in your life and what's on your must-have list. For example, if you require a partner who understands and respects your work ethic, you may want to inquire:

* Is your work a big priority for you?

e-dating Story
Tell me more

I introduced two friends at a party once and graciously left them to get to know each other. Upon leaving I noticed he was obviously smitten. When I followed up the next day to ask her what she talked to him about, she told me she hardly said anything during the whole conversation, "He was so interesting, I just kept asking him to tell me more. I was content to listen to him talk about his life, his work and philosophies all night." When I asked him what he thought of her, he said she was the brightest, most intellectual and stimulating conversationalist he had ever met.

♥ Do you put in a lot of overtime?

Similarly, if a balanced lifestyle is important to you, you'll want to ask your love interest one of the following:

♥ Do you take time for yourself outside work?
♥ What do you like to do to de-stress and relax?
♥ Do you find your work overwhelming sometimes?
♥ How do you balance it with other important things?

Inquire, Don't Conduct an Inquisition

Asking is a delicate matter which requires timing, sensitivity and tact. It's all about seizing the right moment in the flow of the conversation. Of course a conversation should never become an interrogation which dampens the energy and spirit of exploration. When they feel you are genuinely interested in what they have to say or their life, they'll be open to sharing details.

Listen Openly without Judging

Accept whatever they say as defining who they are. Remember, you are asking questions to learn about them. What you learn is only their characteristics. Listen for nervousness, hesitation or creative avoidance of the question, manipulation, denial, distortion, or omission of details. Listen for their reaction to your questions and statements. Listen for life, character, or personality-defining statements like, " I've always believed," or "from my point of view."

TOP 10 GUIDELINES FOR ASKING QUESTIONS

1. Inquire, don't conduct an inquisition. Don't fire questions, let them come up casually in conversation.

2. Use body language that indicates you're interested. (Smile, lean forward, look intently, head tilted, hands open and visible)

3. Use a friendly, pleasant tone of voice when asking. Smile when asking questions (even on the phone); you'll sound less serious.

4. Ask in the positive. Never use phrases like "You wouldn't ...would you?" or "I don't like... Don't you agree?"

5. Ask the tough questions up front. It's usually easier and more comfortable for people to answer when they are still anonymous. The questions you don't ask early may be more difficult to ask later when you are more familiar.

6. Keep control of the conversation flow. If you want to discuss something in particular, bridge or link topics back to what you prefer to discuss.

7. Ask one question at a time, then shut up! Sometimes people need time to consider and elaborate and answer.

8. Listen, Listen, Listen. The answers can sometimes lead to more follow-up questions. Listen actively, give your full attention. People like to feel that you care about what they are sharing. They'll open up even more.

9. Thank them for sharing personal information and express appreciation for their being so honest and upfront. Wherever possible agree with a nod or verbally, it builds trust and rapport.

10. Find common ground and share a personal tidbit that is relevant. Practice "need to know." Get information

before you volunteer information they don't necessarily need to know.

CONTINUING CONVERSATIONS...

There's nothing more uncomfortable than a pregnant pause in a conversation with someone new when neither person knows what to say. This often happens when one person makes a statement and then isn't sure how far to take the conversation or if the other is really interested. People love to talk about themselves; all you need to do is continue the conversation. Here are a few phrases guaranteed to get you out of a jam, whether on the phone or on a first date.

- ♥ That's interesting, tell me more...
- ♥ Really, how so?
- ♥ You think so? I'm not sure...
- ♥ Have you ever considered...?
- ♥ You mentioned...tell me more about...
- ♥ I'm curious about...
- ♥ Can you elaborate further?
- ♥ How do you feel about...?
- ♥ I'm not familiar with that, can you explain it to me?
- ♥ Help me out a bit, would you explain what you mean by...?
- ♥ I'd like to hear more about your thoughts on...
- ♥ When you said.... It made me think of... I was wondering...
- ♥ I'm glad you brought that up, because I've often thought...
- ♥ You said...That's interesting because...
- ♥ What would you like to know about me?

TOP 20 FACT FINDING QUESTIONS

1. What do you do for a living?
2. Where do you work? (Does your company have a website I could visit?)
3. What's your phone number? (Can I reach you at home later?)
4. Where did you grow up? (Home town?)
5. Where did you go to high school?
6. Do you have brothers and sisters? (Ages? Names? Where?)
7. Where do you live now? (Area of town?)
8. Do you own your own home? (Have you ever owned a home? Property? Boat? Car? Business?)
9. Do you live alone?
10. Did you go to college or university? (Where? What was your major?)
11. Have you ever been married? (How many times? Where?)
12. Do you ever want to be married again?
13. Do you have children? (Ages? How do you feel about children?)
14. Do you have pets? (Names?)
15. Do you play sports or outside activities? (On a team?)
16. Do you belong to any clubs, associations and organizations?
17. Tell me about a typical day in the life of you? (Any particular habits or rituals?)
18. What three things do you like to do on your day off? (Where do you like to hang out?)
19. Who's your best friend? (Name? Do you have many friends?)
20. Do you like to travel? (Do you have a passport?)

TOP 20 CHARACTER-TELLING QUESTIONS

1. What would be your ideal relationship? (What are you looking for?)
2. What is the most important compatibility in a relationship? (Lifestyle/social activities, financial, intellectual, sexual, or moral/political compatibility.)
3. What type of things did you learn about yourself in your last relationship?
4. What three things do you value most in life? (Priorities?)
5. Are you a morning person or nocturnal creature?
6. Do you have pet peeves? (What do people do that drives you crazy?)
7. Have you ever had a really embarrassing moment you'd be willing to share?
8. What's your biggest dream or goal? (Where do you see yourself in 10 years?)
9. Are you ambitious? (What does your vision of the future look like?)
10. What are your political leanings? (What issues are you passionate about?)
11. Tell me about your spiritual life? (Do you have faiths or belief in something greater than yourself?)
12. What are the three most important things in a relationship for you?
13. Have you ever been head-over heals in love? (How would you define love?)
14. Do you believe in Destiny? (Fate? Serendipity? Things meant to be?)
15. Would you say you have a competitive type personality or more willing to contribute to a team goal?

16. How important is age difference when dating? (Do you prefer older or younger partners?)
17. How important are racial differences or religious ones?
18. Are you more an extrovert or an introvert?
19. Are you philanthropic? (Do you donate time, energy, or money to your community or charities?)
20. Have you ever told a lie? (When is it ok to tell a lie? White lies?)

TOP 20 BAGGAGE-REVEALING QUESTIONS

1. Do you have a close family? (Keep in touch by phone? Holiday together?)
2. Did you fight much with your siblings? (Other than the normal give and take). Do you get along now?
3. Is there anyone you are not on speaking terms with? (Family, Friends).
4. Tell me about your mother, what's she like? (Good relationship? Speak often?)
5. Tell me about your dad? (What does/did he do? Are you close?)
6. If you feel comfortable...Would you tell me about your ex?
7. How did it end? (Who ended the relationship?)
8. Do you get along today? (How often do you see each other, talk, and socialize?)
9. Have you dated much since your separation/divorce?
10. How do your kids feel about your dating?
11. How do you feel about marriage? (Would you want to get married again?)
12. What are your relationship deal-breakers? (Things you cannot stand?)

13. How do you feel about children? Are you close with your kids now?

14. What do you fear the most?

15. When you get upset or in an argument, how do you usually react? How do you solve it?

16. How important is sex? How often do you like it? Have any inhibitions?

17. What are your financial habits? Do you prefer to save up and pay cash or buy on credit and worry about it next month?

18. Would you say you are a thrifty scrimper, a regular saver, big spender or last-minute scrounger?

19. In money matters, is how much someone earns or who pays an issue for you?

20. Have you ever really been in love?

TOP 20 RED FLAG AND STOP-SIGN QUESTIONS

1. Is your divorce/separation complete?

2. How many serious relationships have you had in your life?

3. Have you ever had sex with someone you barely know?

4. Do you have someone you consider a sex-buddy?

5. Have you ever dated someone who was married? (Had an affair?)

6. Do you have best friends or family members that you tell everything to? (Seek advice from?)

7. How often do you put in overtime? (Have you ever been a workaholic?)

8. Do you ever get jealous or suspicious?

9. Do you get mad or get even? (Do you hold a grudge?)

10. Have you ever threatened anyone physically? (Legally? Threatened to sue?)

11. Have you ever been in a fight since childhood?
12. Have you ever hit a woman/man?
13. Tell me about the last time you got really drunk? (Drink of choice? What are your drinking habits?)
14. Have you ever been in trouble with the law? (Have your friends?)
15. Have you ever had any addictions? (Been in therapy?)
16. Have you ever been treated for depression? (Been prescribed anti-depressants?)
17. Have you ever experimented with recreational drugs? (Do you now? Do your friends do drugs?)
18. Have you ever been fired? (Why?)
19. Have you ever quit a job due to personality differences?
20. Have you ever checked up on someone you were in a relationship with? (Hired a private investigator?)

TOP 20 JUST-FOR-FUN QUESTIONS

1. How far would you travel for a date?
2. Do you believe in love at first sight?
3. Tell me your favourite joke.
4. What is your favourite TV show?
5. Who is your favourite comedian?
6. Who is your favourite musical artist?
7. What's the best concert you've ever been to?
8. If you were a fruit (dog, animal), what would you be? Why?
9. If you could do anything on a first date, what would it be?
10. What type of movie would you take someone on a 2nd date?
11. Are you ticklish? Where?
12. When is it the proper time to kiss someone you have just met? First date? Second date? Third date?

13. What is your favourite body part on someone else? Have you ever eaten chocolate off of it?
14. Have you ever been to an X-rated movie with someone you have been in a relationship with?
15. Have you ever acted out one of the scenes?
16. What's your favourite fantasy/day dream?
17. What is the strangest place you have ever had sex?
18. Have you ever surprised your partner at work wearing only a trench coat and a smile?
19. What's the best/most unique gift you've ever given someone?
20. Have you ever created a romantic weekend for your partner and just whisked them away without them knowing where they are going?

In this chapter...

Secret #8

Be safe rather than sorry... Go Google before you go ga-ga

The conventional dating model is like dating naked. Let's say you agree to go out with someone you met casually through a social event, blind date or in a bar. You're nervous, raw, exposed and unprotected because you really don't know much about the stranger you are dating and it takes several dates to find out.

E-dating is the safest form of dating, if you use your intuition and a little common sense. By doing a little homework first you'll at least know something about whom you are dating. You have the opportunity to pre-screen and pre-qualify your interest so you feel more comfortable and safe before you even lay eyes on each other.

You'll want to refer to this chapter over and over to ensure you're taking the appropriate precautions. If you follow all the steps in this chapter you'll feel more confident, know how to protect yourself and be less likely to find yourself in a dangerous liaison. I have followed these steps myself (along with the Rule of Three) and flown across Canada and the USA to meet many virtual strangers without incident. In fact, I can honestly say I have only had quality experience, and romantic adventures.

DECEPTION HAPPENS

Of course deception happens. The first thing to accept is that deception is virtually guaranteed to one degree or another. Whether intentionally or unintentionally, people lie, cheat and misrepresent themselves. Many internet daters have come across people who use old photos that make them look younger and thinner. I've met men on the internet who confessed after the second phone call that they posted their age as under fifty because they thought they'd get more responses from younger chicks. Another waited until the second date to tell

e-dating Story

It should be common sense

Steve met a woman in a chat room who suggested he drive to the next city to meet her next weekend. After a few phone conversations, she even offered to let him stay overnight. When he reached the city limits, he called to say he was running late. Apparently, she had a case of nerves, told him she was going for a walk and left him a key to let himself in. It boggles the mind how a thirty-something, classically educated, professional woman would give a total stranger she's never met a key to her home. She left him there alone for over an hour with free time to rummage around her personal belongings, not to mention give opportunity for theft. Even more surprising was that she really did have him stay the whole weekend. They enjoyed each other and discovered they weren't a match. Lucky for her he was a man of honour. However, there are smarter ways to meet for the first time without leaving oneself vulnerable to potential thieves, sexual predators and stalkers.

me his divorce wasn't final and his ex was still living under the same roof!

Whether it's pretending to be someone they are not or withholding key pieces of information until the "right moment," you're not likely to get the whole story up front. But that shouldn't make you sceptical; it should only make you more careful and better at asking questions.

One of the myths about online dating is that the internet is only for liars, losers, lonely-hearts and lusty old men. I've had my share of fakes, frauds and phonies but not any more than you would meeting someone casually in a bar. The truth is, the vast majority of online daters are ordinary, genuine and honest people like you.

- ❦ "You look at this picture day after day, then when you meet them it's an automatic downer because you realize you've been deceived. Did she really think I wasn't going to notice?"

- ❦ "A few men told me they were 5'11, but when we met it was obvious they were closer to 5'7. I'm a tall woman and it's not that I can't love a shorter man, but I certainly can't love a liar who's not confident in himself."

It's a natural tendency to embellish or paint a picture of what we wish we were and omit negative traits and inconvenient facts. Most people do it unconsciously. In reality, how we see ourselves is much different (positively and negatively) from how others see us. Don't expect the worst but keep your eyes open and look for the best, which someone may not be confident enough to tell you.

ASK LOTS OF QUESTIONS AND VERIFY THE ANSWERS

Asking the right questions is Secret #7, and you'll find many helpful suggestions to play 20 questions in chapter 7.

You can't always trust someone you meet online, but you can always trust your gut.

~ Stephany

If you want a real reference guide you can keep on hand so you're never at a loss for questions, look for the next book of this series, e-dating *Secrets Questions* — From Icebreakers to Deal-breakers Questions Everyone Should Ask *Before* Falling in Love.

When it comes to safety you'll want to focus on the fact-finding questions and keep notes in your e-dating *Secrets* Journal (available at *www.e-datingexperts.com*), then look for ways to verify the answers. One way to do this is to ask checking questions. Your goal is to see if you get the same answer twice. One way is to deliberately fudge a fact in casual conversation and wait for them to correct you. For instance, you can say, "Didn't you tell me you worked for XYZ Company, what's that like?" Or if you know the company he/she works for is in the east end of town, try a checking question something like, "You mentioned before you worked in the west end of town, do you live there, too?" The point is, someone who has fibbed will likely not remember what they told you or won't bother to correct you.

Another great idea is to find a bull-buster buddy. Ask a friend to double date and have him or her ask the same questions to see if they get the same answers. Although I don't recommend deception, I have also heard of women being thorough and teaming up with a friend to write the same guy to verify if he is sincere, if he writes the same responses or answers the same way. Obviously you'd have to trust that your friend would end contact at some point and leave the prospect to you for a date. You'll also have to think about how to answer and justify this set up when he/she finds out you are friends.

PRACTICE "NEED TO KNOW"

Practicing "Need to Know" could be the most important secret of online dating, especially for women. It basically means, "I need to know and you don't." You should feel free to ask many questions but be very careful about the amount of personal information you give, and only answer the important questions.

Obviously, if everyone plays it too close to the vest, then no one would know anything about anyone and that defeats the purpose. At some point when you are very comfortable and assured that you may have a match, you'll begin to reveal some personal information, but until then, the name of the game is ask for as much detailed personal information as nonchalantly as you can and reveal very little of your own personal details. This is much easier for women to do than men, as men generally have a "no big deal" attitude and are more open and less threatened about revealing details. If you're a guy wooing a woman, expect to do some significant wooing before you get the goods on her.

Most e-daters know not to give out personal information, yet it's amazing how many do it anyway. Giving out information about where you work or spend leisure time can be dangerous. For instance, knowing that a woman works at a particular company and plays golf in a certain city can lead to someone showing up at her place of employment. Knowing approximately where she lives and part of her name can yield her home address.

There are thousands of databases available online which

can be used to find someone's home address. Most States have a registry of deeds which is automated and searchable. These allow someone to find out what property is owned by almost anyone. Many states have their vehicle license registry available for sale to online database companies, many include photographs and some even include social security numbers. A predator who knows part of your name, and approximately where you live (even just the State can be sufficient), can match your photograph from the dating website to a photograph from the State's Department of Motor Vehicles and get your home address.

PROTECT YOUR PHONE NUMBER

While uninvited calls can be annoying, a phone number can lead to uninvited and unexpected visitors. With a first name and a telephone number it doesn't take much for someone to find out where you live, and/or get more information that could lead to identity theft.

It's a good idea to use a separate unlisted telephone number for e-dating. Some people find it more comfortable to use their cell phone with the caller ID blocked. However, for a few extra dollars per month most phone companies have a special "Identi-Call" or "Ring Mate" line that allow you to add a second or third phone number to your existing line which has a distinctive ring. This way you'll know by the ring if it is a date calling and if the number gets abused you can simply cancel or request a new number.

You can ask your phone company to have your telephone number unlisted or have your caller ID blocked permanently. However if your number is in the phone book, there's really no point.

If you're a woman, the alternative is to arrange a specific

time to call by email then call him. You can enter a code (*82 in most States and *67 in Canada) before you dial each call so your number is blocked. These services typically cost 25 to 50 cents per call.

Most men will understand and respect women taking care of personal safety. This is the modern dating reality; no one will think you're paranoid.

CAN YOU BE TOO CAREFUL?

There are thousands of horror stories in newspapers across North America about young girls being seduced into a clandestine meeting by a chat-room stalker and women disappearing after having engaged in online relationships. There are stories about women being seduced by liars, cheats, married men and even by men still in the slammer. There an equal number of stories of men being seduced by fatal-attraction-like stalkers, but they don't make the papers as often. The point is, the anonymity of the internet makes it the ideal playground for people with sinister intentions, and you can't be too careful.

e-dating Story

Uninvited and unexpected

There was a guy I had great conversations with online, but by the third date I knew there was no chemistry in it for me. I thought I was very clear when I broke it off over the phone. He seemed disappointed, but said he understood that's the way it is sometimes and wished me well. Two weeks after we ended it, he showed up at my doorstep unannounced one morning before I left for work to confront me saying he was confused and it something was incomplete. It was unnerving and creepy because I don't remember telling him where I lived and had never invited him to my home. We talked, we hugged and I never saw him again, but I'm much more careful now.

TOP 10 E-DATING SAFETY TIPS

1. *Stay Anonymous*
   It's perfectly acceptable to stay on a first name basis for

the first few online en-
counters until you feel
completely comfortable. I
chose not to give out my
first name until the first
date and would often cor-

Bottom line — you are who you are and you want them to love you for whom you are, so don't be shy about it.

~ Stephany

respond with my catchy profile name or initial. It would drive men crazy with curiosity and intrigue, and it worked.

2. *Un-list and Block Your Home Telephone Number*
   Remember, it's not hard for someone to find an address and other personal information when they have a name or phone number.

3. *Keep a Journal*
   Keep track of names, dates, places, details, conversations and experiences. You can scribble notes on profiles or use the e-dating Secrets'™ Journal which is based on the rule of three and keep it all in one place.

4. *Use a Cell Phone*
   Carry a cell phone with you at all times for additional safety. If it has a GPS locator built in, even better!

5. *Tell a Friend or Family Member*
   When it comes to e-dating, your mother's rule applies at any age. Make sure you tell someone where you are going, who you are with and what time you expect to be back. You may not need a babysitter or curfew, but for women it is good personal safety.

6. *Meet Someplace Public*

    Choose a neutral and familiar, public place not too close
    to home.

7. *Arrange a Double Date or Drop-by*

    Ask a friend to join you for a double date, to drop by or
    accidentally bump into you during your date. You'll wel-
    come the second opinion and/or the good company if the
    date turns out to be a disaster.

8. *Have a Quick Exit and Back-up Plan*

    One of my friends who is used to being on-call for work
    asks me to call her 2 hours into her new date so she can
    make a quick exit if she has to. Work out a signal with a
    friend either in person or by phone that will let them
    know if you prefer to continue the date alone or be res-
    cued and go home.

9. *Drive Yourself*

    Don't let your date pick you up or drive you home. Take a
    cab or get a friend to drive you if necessary

10. *Use Your Intuition*

    We all have a sixth sense or intuition. The challenge most
    of us have is listening to it. There are bound to be times
    when you can't really put your finger on it. It's not
    something specific that he said or she did, but you still
    have an uncomfortable, uneasy feeling. Don't ignore
    the little hairs on the back of your neck...Click delete and
    say "Next."

HOW MUCH SHOULD I REVEAL?

I once heard another online dating coach caution women not to share their personal goals, dreams, career paths, or vision of the future until they've dated at least 5 months. I would argue just the opposite. Of course caution should be taken in the beginning not to reveal details that may compromise your safety. But when it comes to philosophies of life, preferences, vision for where you're headed in life and things you feel strongly about, why waste 5 months before you find out he/she really can't stand that about you? I believe in getting very clear and confident in knowing who you are and how you choose to live and then being as upfront as possible about it.

7 THINGS YOU SHOULD NEVER REVEAL UNTIL AFTER THE THIRD DATE

1. *Personal Email Address*
   Spam artists and scam artists love your personal email. Always use an anonymous hotmail or yahoo account that is separate from all your other email and only for online dating. You're likely to be spammed out of it eventually but it's also a safer bet in case an online date goes sour.

2. *Full Name*
   Identity thieves don't need much information to take advantage. Even a middle initial or maiden name can be a key that unlocks doors to information and new identities. It's always better to avoid helping them use you. It's acceptable to stay on a first name basis or use your nickname or online alias.

3. *Home Telephone Number*
   Avoid the risk of inconvenient or harassing phone calls. Remember, a phone number is sometimes all it takes to find an address.

4. *Home Address*
   Until you are dating exclusively, you don't want the embarrassment of unexpected or inconvenient visits, not to mention the potential for information to be used or passed on by stalkers and sales people.

5. *Company and Location of Work*
   An unexpected or embarrassing visit at work is only second to one at home. No one is worth the risk of losing your job.

6. *Details about Your Children (names, ages, where they go to school etc.)*
   Don't make your children vulnerable. It's ok to include a photo of you and your kids and refer to them by pet names, but details about their

names, where they go to school and play are not details anyone "needs to know." Raise an eyebrow if you are asked.

7. *Places, Restaurants or Stores You Frequent*
People with sinister motives want to know where you are and where you move. Don't let anyone know your patterns until you are ready to include them.

GO GOOGLE TO GATHER THE GOODS

It's almost scary what you can find out about people on the internet. Most people would be shocked at the amount of personal information that is available in the public domain. Not only can you find websites, email, telephone numbers and family history, but if you've had any dealings in the public, corporate sector or community

e-dating Story
Big, bold and beautiful

Of course I don't believe any lady should ever have to reveal her weight and any guy who asks lacks tact and class. But on the internet, guys sometimes get nervous. One online suitor had just had a negative experience and told me he just learned the true meaning of "full figured" and "big boned" the hard way. He said he never really understood women's sizes before he was duped by women online.

Having been previously obese and very proud of my weight loss (65lbs), I am by no means ashamed of the way I look. However, I am still somewhat naturally conscious of my weight. So I felt challenged as to how much I would tell him before we met for the first time. I thought about it awhile and became concerned that he might be looking for a petite bikini model, which I am most definitely not. I made a decision to do something most women never do... I actually sent him a very tasteful swimsuit photo and included my measurements with a playful humorous note of reassurance and a little Mae West attitude.

continued on p. 153...

service, trade or alumni organizations, there's likely more information posted about you out there. To convince yourself, try doing a search on your own name or variations of it and see what comes up. The first time I searched my name and city I was surprised to find listings of my previous businesses, newspaper articles about my political life, charitable causes I supported and conferences where I spoke or attended. There were even articles I wrote about holistic health ten years ago which were still posted on someone else's website.

e-dating Story

...continued from p. 152

This move was as much a test of my confidence as it was a test for him to accept me as I am. And it worked! He was blown away and very impressed with my honesty. He sent back a very complimentary and very validating note indicating how sexy he thought I was. It made all the difference getting that out of the way before our first meeting so both of us knew exactly what to expect.

Once you've casually collected notes and names of your love interests home town, education, workplace, the names of family, business partners, best friends, etc...Google! Go to *www.google.com*, it's one of the largest or visit any big search engine and do advanced searches on multiple terms including, city, full names, etc. You may have to play around with initials and short form spellings of their name to find what you are looking for, but it will be well worth it. The hard part is narrowing down your search to get relevant information. Google is actually smart enough to know which country you are coming in from and adjusts the site to your specific locale.

When I started online dating, Google.com became my best friend. I would check out company websites, associations and alumni lists, not just to verify what was told to me in conversation, but also to learn juicy tidbits of information that I could use in conversation. Most of the time, men were surprised at how much I knew about them. One said he was flattered that I was interested enough to have done my homework and learn something about who he was and intelligent enough to check up for my own personal safety.

ARE THEY WHO THEY SAY THEY ARE? DO A BACKGROUND CHECK

E-dating *Experts* do not believe you need to do a background check on every love interest. However, if you want peace of mind, before you get too seriously involved you should check out some of the facts in someone's story, at least until you are satisfied that they're telling the truth. You can find a lot of information yourself in about an hour over the internet.

e-dating Story
Don't date blind online
A friend once set me up for a blind date with a self-made millionaire. We exchanged online profiles, talked on the phone and he flew to meet me. It really never occurred to me to follow my own rules in this case, so I took him and my friend's endorsement at face value. Our date went well enough, and although not convinced we were a match, I agreed to keep in touch.

Arriving home, I received a disturbing email from his ex-wife who had found my profile and emails at his home computer. She said I reminded her of herself, with an uncanny resemblance to her as a single mom. She had met him online, had a whirlwind romance, married, moved and had a child. Only after things went sour did she begin doing a background search in public record in various places of his past. She claimed wild stories of a wealthy first wife that she believed died under mysterious circumstances, a second wife unhappy because her

continued on p. 155...

Details You Can Search Yourself on the Internet for Free

1. *Telephone Numbers and Addresses*
   There are many sites which can help you find personal and business telephone numbers and addresses. The easiest

is to visit *www.411.com* or *www.411.ca.* You can even do a reverse lookup of someone's telephone number if you don't have a full name.

2. *Previous Associations*
   If someone claims to be involved with a charity, service organization, professional networking group or association you can usually find a website or a published membership guide that will list their name or profile, donation or awards recognition.

3. *Political Associations*
   All political donations over $200 are recorded and reported in Canada and the US. You can find contributions of any individual or business to any political party or candidate by region or last name through the Secretary of State's office or Elections Canada Website, www.elections.ca

e-dating Story

...continued from p. 154
husband loved money more than her and kept control of every cent.

She told stories of her husband parading affairs with strippers in and out of the home regardless of the presence of children. She claimed everything was verifiable through court and state records if I cared to research and talk with ex-wives and friends as she did. I dismissed her credibility when she confessed to having access to his home and still loving him enough to share a bed and sex regularly.

I dismissed him as less than truthful when he confessed to being in the middle of a custody battle and wanted to involve me with lawyers. Apparently, they did not have an amicable relationship as he had previously told me. When he contacted me again I told him my bottom line: I did not know him well enough to judge where the truth lay, but it was obviously complicated and incomplete. These things have a way of working themselves out for the best. I wished him well. I did not want to be involved and I had no time, patience or inclination for that level of drama in my life.

4. *If someone has a small business*

Check the small business registry, local papers, the better business bureau, the local chamber of commerce list of members, call the local library. You can also check most federal and state business registries online. For corporations info in Canada go to *http://strategis.ic.gc.ca*

5. *Recent articles about a person*

Some articles will come up on a Google.com search but you can also search on website archives of local papers of the city in which the person lives in. In Canada, you can do an extensive search of all media at *www.financial-post.infomart.ca*

6. *Local Public Records*

Although privacy legislation does limit the amount of public information you can get in some provinces and states, court records are usually public. There is a great deal of information still available through registrars or your local Municipal records office. Some public libraries have access to Lexus/Nexus research information which indexes all major news sources and most Court cases.

Should You Hire Someone to Do a Background Check?

This is a personal question that must be asked, but if you think that the person you are dealing with is not on the up and up, perhaps you should simply listen to your instincts and just end it first.

If you get to the point where you are seriously thinking about uprooting your life for a long distance love, it may be worth it. For $30-$100 you can get a full report listing everything from criminal records, bankruptcies, court records or public records of business and corporate information.

To conduct a background check on someone, all you need is their Name and Present/Previous Address, Date of Birth or Social Security Number. There are a lot of internet services that have the ability to search public information and some government databases. It's like hiring a private detective to search all the public records for you. You'll likely save more time and money than trying to do it yourself.

When e-dating*Experts*.com did a search on Google.com, it came up with over 630,000 sites on how to get information about people. They were either free sites or a combination of free and pay.

Please note that E-dating *Experts* does not endorse any one service in particular, as we cannot guarantee the quality of services, privacy or prices. The results from various services are often inconsistent. Keep in mind that these services only report what is public record. This means you may end up paying for a report only to have it say that there are no results for this request. We recommend you check a company out thoroughly before you buy a report.

There are some websites which currently offer some free reports and information such as *www.knowx.com*, but like any-

---

thing else you usually get what you pay for, so check out a portal like *www.peoplespot.com* for links to many different public records sites like *www.publicrecords.com* or

www.ussearch.com

Online Services Can Provide Important Details

- AKA's — All names previously associated with an individual (Including birth and previous married names.)
- Relatives/ Ancestry/ Birth/Death Records
- Address Profiles (Current/Past)
- National Voter Registration Records
- Real Property / Land Ownership Records (Purchase dates, amount, value)
- Automobile Registration Records
- U.S Postal Service Change of Address
- National Marketing Databases
- Magazine Subscription Lists
- DMV (Drivers License Information In States Where Available)
- Accident Records and Reports
- Aircraft/Watercraft Ownership
- Professional Licenses (Certifications)
- Current National Telephone Listings
- Former National Telephone Listings
- Corporate Affiliations/Associates
- Government/Federal Contracts

- Domain Name Registration
- Bankruptcy Filings/Judgements
- UCC Filings
- Civil Litigation (Court) Records
- Marriage/Divorce Records
- Civil Judgements/Liens
- Tax Liens
- Deed Transfers

In this chapter...

See the signs, use your intuition, reject without rejecting

There will be people who write to you that you feel are not the right match from the start. There will be times you share a few telephone conversations and decide you don't want to meet in person. There will be people you meet in person that you just don't click with. Ending an online relationship is less complicated and much easier than conventional dating. Goodbyes are as easy as a Dear John email.

HOW TO REJECT SOMEONE
WITHOUT THEM FEELING REJECTED

If you discover you're not an ideal match, the best thing to do is to tell them so, kindly. There is no need to go into details or point out faults that may hurt someone's feelings. If you know right away that this person is not a match, you can simply say so.

It doesn't cost anything to be kind and respectful and leave someone feeling good about their contact with you. Once you get used to the formula it becomes quick and easy to read someone's profile and compose a personal note. A few times I received very poetic notes from men who didn't find me their type, and I felt flattered they took the time. Other times, when I was the one ending the liaison with a kind note, men would send a second note saying, "That was the nicest Dear John letter I ever received," thanking me for being honest. There are a couple of sample responses that follow the formula.

When e-dating you have to remember, people often come on with life-long intentions and leave with the click of a mouse.

~ Stephany

Dear John,

Thank you very much for your heartfelt note and compliments about my profile.

I enjoyed reading your profile and seeing your photos.

The photos of you and your dog were fun to see.

You're obviously a man with a romantic heart and you know what you want in life.

However, I do not believe we are an ideal match.

I'm sure there's a special woman out there who will truly appreciate what your heart has to offer.

Enjoy the journey,

Dear Suzy,

Thank you for responding to my profile. I was flattered by your compliments.

Your profile was very well written.

I can tell you approach life with intelligence, humour and a great attitude.

I recently began exploring possibilities with someone else I met online.

To be fair, I'd prefer to give her a chance and see where it leads.

I know it won't be long before you find the lucky guy who is going to capture your attention.

Best of luck in your search for "the one,"

Reality Check

Let them down easy in four simple steps

1. Thank them and express appreciation
2. Compliment them about who they are
3. Decline gracefully and clearly
4. Wish them well in continuing their search

TOP 20 DEAR JOHN (OR JANE) EXCUSES

1. "I don't feel I fit the profile of the person you're looking for."
2. "I'd prefer not to date long-distance and will continue my search locally."
3. "Your children are adorable; however, I'm not a family-oriented person."
4. "I'm seeking someone with a similar ethnic and spiritual background."
5. "I have children and prefer to find someone who's looking to settle down."
6. "I don't believe we have enough in common to share a

future or be compatible long-term."

7. "It seems you are looking a for more serious relationship than I am capable of at this time."

8. "Although I like animals, I'm allergic to cats and that would make our dating too complicated."

9. "My work keeps me on the road, and I'd prefer not to have to travel to date someone."

10. "You seek adventure with someone, and I'm afraid I'm not really the adventurous type."

11. "I don't believe that we have the kind of chemistry that I'm looking for."

12. "Your car engine revs a little too fast for me."

13. "It's apparent to me your relationship (or divorce) is not yet complete."

14. "I'm looking for someone who is not tied down and is open to moving if they find the love of their life."

15. "I'd prefer not to date a smoker."

16. "Our tastes appear too different to mix in the same soup."

17. "I prefer to date someone closer to my age."

e-dating Story
Some people's children!

I emailed a beautiful woman that had a very descriptive profile. She was young, and to me that is taking a larger chance on someone who might not know what they want or who might prove to be really immature. So I get a few responses back from her, the last one made me decide to give her a chance. She wrote something like "I have read your profile and I really like who you say you are." She asked if we could meet and said that she wanted to be in a serious relationship. She willingly gave me her phone number a couple of times. So I sent an email to let her know I would take her up on a phone call and would like to meet her. She emailed right back saying, "Oh, I re-read your profile and I hate children. I absolutely hate children!" She felt it was better not to call or meet. How could she miss the fact that I have three children I adore? Their pictures are in my profile and this was after 4 emails!

18. "I'm looking for someone with few obligations and the freedom to travel."
19. "I'd prefer to date someone with a similar career and goals."
20. "I'm looking for a more serious relationship leading to marriage."

TOP 10 REASONS NOT TO RESPOND TO A PROFILE

There are some legitimate reasons not to respond to someone's profile or email. For instance, if they do not post a photo and refuse to send you one upon request, you should suspect something. Personal safety should be a concern if someone asks for personal information and wants to take the conversation offline immediately to meet in person. They may not be single at all if they refuse to answer or avoid sharing details of their lifestyle and living circumstance.

1. There is no photo attached to the profile or they do not send you one upon request.
2. There are fewer than 6-8 lines in their profile blurb.
3. You receive a wink, smile, or teaser but no intro email.
4. The email is a form letter or they have obviously not read (or mentioned) my profile.
5. The profile is attached to email with no note.
6. The profile is generic, boring or two lines.
7. What they are looking for is listed as "Any" or "All" or "I'll tell you later."

8. They request a messenger chat without an introductory email first.
9. They request a date or personal information in the first email.
10. They don't meet your personal must-have and can't-stand list.

PATTERNS OF ONLINE SEEKERS

The online dating world is very much like the conventional dating world; there are people ready for mature relationship and others who are not. As humans mature into different life stages and types of relationships there are stereotypical patterns that emerge. Once you've online dated awhile you'll discover the online dating world has its own unique patterns or stages of maturity which parallel common real-life love patterns. It's helpful to consider them and keep your eyes open so you don't end up wasting your time with the wrong person.

Stage One: Puppy Love

First-time e-daters are usually flattered, overwhelmed and thrilled by the volume of genuine responses they get. This stage is like our first childhood puppy love. It's common for newcomers to e-dating to get carried away and jump in head first, confessing everything, telling their life stories. They tend to fall for the first one or two they meet online and presume a "too good to be true" relationship too soon.

Stage Two: Confident Cruiser

Once people have been online for a while they start to see there are lots of fish in the sea. They get more responses and get a confidence or ego boost. After all, with this many people interested they must be really hot stuff, right? I compare this to the way we felt when we started discovering how attractive we were to the opposite sex and began adolescently seeking the attention. The Confident Cruisers are just out there having fun, meeting new people, sometimes posting on multiple sites for multiple hits.

Stage Three: Playful Player

After cruising awhile people sometimes become "players." They tend to generate entertaining and meaningless conversation and often experiment to discover how far they can push boundaries, what kind of sexy thrills they can create with different people, much like we do during hormone-induced explorations in college.

Players like to push buttons with sexual innuendo, racy photos and steamy phone sex to create dead-end adventures that become intense and confused relationships or notches on bedposts and great stories for the memoirs.

Stage Four: Serious Surfer

Eventually people get bored with game playing, like we do in our thirties. We've been there, done that and get serious and more discriminating in our dating adventures. Serious Surfers have figured out who they are and what they want. They rewrite their profiles, are more relaxed about dating and have a more relaxed approach. They have had enough online experience to know how to read between the lines and avoid pitfalls. They know what they want, they're determined and on target to find it.

BEWARE the Serial Dater

The serial daters are the ones that get stuck in the middle-aged muddle. They are addicted to endless dating. They love dating and realize that there are lots of fish in the sea, often chasing too many fish, never really getting too attached because they know there are always more fish in the sea. This is most common with the recently divorced.

Sometimes the serial daters are really just commitment-phobic or chronic daters. They get close to someone, realize they've opened up and made themselves emotionally vulnerable, but they never seem to take it to the next level of in-person dating. For some, internet dating is good therapy until they figure out what they really want and become Serious Surfers. Others, say they want a serious relationship and have no problem getting to the first, second, third date, but then resist taking in their shingle or hiding their profile when it's time to commit to dating exclusively. They're always wondering if there is someone better out there. After all, there are millions to choose from, right?

The Sex Surfer

The final pattern is the one many online daters fear. I haven't come across sexual predators personally, but I have come across stories of men and women who only seem to want phone sex or hot and steamy messenger chats. You can recognize them because they usually ask for your phone number right away because they want to hear your sexy voice, or they instant messenger you with "what are you wearing?" The Sexy Surfer only has one intention, to get beyond the chat room to the bedroom as fast as possible. Once that happens, the thrill is gone and they move on. Instead of surfing the sites dedicated to people who are easy and looking for a walk on the wild side, they choose the challenge of finding someone on a romance site.

BOTTOM LINE ADVICE ON GETTING TO RELATIONSHIP

In general, you have about 90 days to close the online "get to know each other" phase and move to a first date in person. This is especially true if it's long distance. If you're local it should take less than a week or two. Typically, if you drag on with friendly chatting and phone calls and don't get to a first date, one or both of you will lose interest or it becomes too awkward to get to actually meeting in person. It's not uncommon to receive a letter like the following: "A year later, I thought I'd say hello. I really miss the great conversations we used to have. I've been in a revolving door of first dates, none of them as interesting or as beautiful as you are. I regret not having tried harder to meet you in person. It's just that we seemed have quite a strong connection. I guess it's easier to get to know somebody in driving distance. I'm happy you found someone and wish you all the best. I still think it would be fun to meet someday. Please let me know when or if you ever become 'unattached' again."

WATCH FOR RED FLAGS AND STOPS SIGNS

When things go sour in a relationship, it's usually because we've failed (or refused) to see the signs. We've all heard people say things like, "I knew it, I just didn't want to know it," or "I should have known, I saw it right from the beginning, but I didn't want to believe it." Sometimes, it's because we prefer to see the good in people and give them the benefit of the doubt. Other times, we are so used to being treated a certain way that we fool ourselves into thinking it's normal. No matter what the justification, if we choose to ignore red flags, we have no one to blame but ourselves when things don't work out.

Most of these signs can be seen within 3 dates and should not be ignored, because they are virtually guaranteed to result in unhappy relationships and failure. Of course what you choose to do when you see these signs is your choice. We encourage you to draw the line in the sand, value yourself and your sanity and hold out for the relationship that you deserve. The following is a brief checklist of early warning signs that should raise an eyebrow or make you consider ending the relationship sooner than later.

You Should Be Concerned if You Are Dating Someone Who...

- is constantly negative or cynical about the world and people in general.
- has a consistent attitude of, "I'm OK, it's the rest of the world that's crazy."
- argues often believing he/she is right; does not genuinely listen to others' point of view.
- compliments or charms someone socially, then gossips or expresses negative opinions privately.
- showers extreme affection, attention and/or gifts.
- needs to speak to you many times a day; thinks about you 24 hours per day.
- doesn't call or initiate communication; waits for you to call.

- doesn't make decisions, rather leaves it "up to you" all time.
- has difficulty showing or expressing fear or vulnerability.
- puts on a happy face; pretends everything is fine when something is obviously wrong.
- has difficulty standing up for themselves or setting boundaries when others try to take advantage.
- does not listen openly to your point of view or respect your boundaries.
- is prone to recurring financial difficulties, patterns of debts, bankruptcies, unpaid bills or "tough times."
- won't reveal details of family background.
- doesn't see or speak to family much except on holidays.
- is too influenced by family; talks to them about everything, allowing them to heavily influence choices.
- has a good friend or family member with whom they refuse to talk or resolve issues.
- harbours anger or resentment toward past lovers; make unkind or judgemental comments about them.
- has nothing nice to say about the ex or has only unhappy memories.
- has an unhealthy or non-existent relationship with children.
- still has frequent contact with one or several ex's; talks on the phone with them often; goes out with them occasionally; doesn't include you or involve you in events where the ex may be.
- gives inappropriate attention to other women/men in your presence; engages in excessive flirting.
- needs to be the center of attention and attract sexual advances.

- makes condescending remarks about other women (or men) being weak or incapable, or calls them names like bitch, stupid, lunatic, idiot, etc.
- is prone to excessive partying; thinks it's OK to be drunk or use recreational drugs.
- uses alcohol or drugs (prescription or recreational) daily or to excess.
- brags about bad deeds, practical jokes or what a rebel they used to be.
- must be in charge, have his/her way; sulks or withdraws when not in control.
- automatically assume control of every circumstance; exerts pressure on others.
- refuses to admit mistakes or apologise when proven wrong.
- confesses to bouts of jealousy, trying to manipulate your social interaction.
- reacts strongly when you talk with the opposite sex or mention a friend of the opposite sex; tries to interfere; is possessive or jealous.
- threatens to hit or hurt someone else in conversation; expresses a desire for revenge against someone else.
- acts superior about what he/she would do in your place, always trying to lecture or teach you something; preaches to you about what's right.

In this chapter...

Use the rule of three ...everything good happens in threes

One sure kiss of death for the online dating relationship is getting too serious too fast and expecting too much. You're better off going with the flow, enjoying the excitement, but lowering your expectations and then being pleasantly surprised. The most important thing you can do is release your attachment to the outcome. Keep a realistic attitude, and let the other know it's OK to continue exploring what might be.

While most challenges can be overcome when you fall in love, it's good to be realistic in the beginning. Rather than getting swept away by what if's or swept off your feet by a smooth talker, remind yourself of the possibility that the chemistry may not be right in person, there may not be a practical fit with values and spiritual beliefs, or perhaps there may not be a structural fit in terms of distance, work schedules, children, parents, etc.

Don't expect an immediate response. Many people who online date use an email account that they only check a couple of times per week. If you write daily wondering why they haven't responded yet, you'll not only look too eager or desperate, you'll likely scare them off with your intensity.

Guys should realize that there are far more men than women on most sites and women get many more times the responses than men. She'll likely need a little time to wade through the responses to find her man. Men should also remember that the old social convention of "the guys do the chasing" is still very true on the internet. Guys, if your email box isn't overflowing, just get out there and write to your dream girl; she's probably waiting for you to make the first move.

WHAT'S NEXT?

One of the biggest questions people have when exploring a new online relationship is, "What's the appropriate next step?" You may have become very enamoured with each other, you enjoy time together, you talk every day, you can't get enough of each other and you can't wait to see each other again. It's a natural tendency to want to make him or her yours and take it to the next level. One of the biggest dangers is becoming possessive or demanding exclusivity before the relationship has matured. Knowing when is the trickiest part of all to figure out so you don't offend the other.

THE E-DATING RULE OF THREE

3 Months of Surfing

So you're ready to select a site and post a profile. Many people figure they'll just try it for a month and see what happens.

Worse yet, some bounce around from site to site. We recommend giving a site an honest try for at least 3 months. It usually takes a few weeks to get used to the site features, refine and add to your profile and search the database for potential matches. It's likely that you'll start exploring possibilities with a special someone before the month is up and you'll have to renew anyway just to keep the conversation going. Save yourself a little aggravation by signing up for at least three months. For most sites the monthly fee is the most expensive option. Many sites give you a discount if you subscribe to their premium services for more than three months and let you cancel at any time. You've got nothing to lose.

3 Prospects

Don't juggle more than 3 date prospects at a time. Most people try to juggle too many and have difficulty keeping them straight. It's acceptable (and usually understood) to interact with more than one and even date more than one before you become exclusive. Be straight, be honest about dating others and don't string them along. Record facts and conversations in your e-dating Journal or your head will hurt trying to keep them straight. As soon as you sense there's not a fit, let them know and move on.

3 Emails

Exchange at least three email letters to everyone who interests you. Sometimes people get excited and may want to meet right away, but you'll save time and energy if you keep the relationship online until you're reasonably sure that there's enough compatibility to carry a conversation and have a fun time together.

3 Questions

Ask at least three key questions per email/conversation/date aimed at discovering compatibility. When online dating, asking lots of questions is not

It's better to be dumped after 3 dates than after 3 years.

~ Stephany

considered "nosy," it's an essential sign of interest. How else can you get to know each other? If you do run into someone who is uncomfortable answering questions, you should consider it a red flag and ask yourself if you really want to date them. To be safe, never rush out the door to meet someone who won't reveal details or talk about themselves.

3 Phone Calls

Have at least three phone calls before you decide to meet in person. This will be the first live gauge of what the chemistry is like. You'll see how you communicate and connect, and your prospects openness to questions. You'll also notice the level of comfort between you. Make notes in your e-dating Journal. To be safe, women shouldn't give out their telephone number until after they're comfortable dating this person regularly. Instead, agree by email or messenger on a phone date and time, then initiate the calls yourself. Some people prefer to use their cell phone so their home numbers and addresses can't be traced through directories. We recommend you use an un-listed number and/or call your phone company to block your number from Call Display devices.

3 Dates

The three-date rule states that by the end of the third date you should have a pretty good idea as to whether you could see yourself spending the rest of your life with someone. That's not to say you will, or that you should expect that he or she is "the one." Of course, sometimes you can tell after the first date that you absolutely could not see yourself with someone long term. But remember, first dates are naturally awkward. Unless it's a disaster or he's a real dog, decide now to date at least three times to give it a chance. If you've been dating in cyberspace for awhile it may take a date or two to make the transition to being comfortable in real life. You may be pleasantly surprised by the second or third date to discover that there really is great chemistry.

Dating should be as easy as counting 1-2-3. The three-date rule saves headaches and potential heartache. Within three dates, you should know if you could see yourself spending the rest of your life with someone. If so, great! Explore possibilities for three weeks to three months or more. If not, pick the next three.

~ Stephany

- ❧ Date one: Do we have enough connection to continue exploring possibilities?
- ❧ Date two: Do we have enough in common? Is there enough chemistry?
- ❧ Date three: Am I comfortable continuing to date? Are there any significant red flags? Could I see myself with this person long term?

3 Weeks

Give it at least 3 weeks of quality time together before you become exclusive and take in your internet shingle. With so many fish in the sea, what's the rush? Be honest with those who contact you that you are currently dating someone else, and be honest with your date. Then you can decide together if it feels right for you both to hide your profiles and explore each other exclusively.

3 Weeks – 3 Months before Sex

Don't risk becoming lust-blind and forgetting to ask the tough questions of your virtual stranger. Of course, your values are yours to decide. But practically all experts agree that sex on a first date is never a good idea. It gives the wrong impression and can lead to emotional attachments for which you may not be ready. Once emotions are grounded in physical intimacy, the blinders go on and we tend to ignore the little signs or avoid asking real questions out of discomfort or fear that we may be hurt by the answers. This is one rule that can help avoid potential heartache down the road.

SEX... LOVE AND LUST BLINDNESS

You've met somebody you're interested in, so you rush to your email inbox and find an email like this: "The more I discover about you, the more I realize there is so much more to love. I'm amazed that I can feel you so intensely even though we haven't even met yet. I'm so filled with thoughts of you, I look at your photos and think about what it will be like to touch you and caress you. I wish to know every inch of you inside and out. I'd like to take you to my favourite place overlooking the ocean. It's quiet and secluded, only you and me with a glass of wine on a blanket in front of a captivating sunset. I imagine running my fingers through your hair and slowly kissing your neck. As my fingers descend around your buttocks and across your thigh, my lips will follow your shoulder and taste every inch of you. I want to make you tingle with excitement until your lips quiver and the anticipation overwhelms you with desire..."

Can you feel how exhilarating it might be to get an email like this while exploring a new relationship or love interest? You feel desired and desirable. The anticipation of your next connection builds with intensity, puts a smile on your face and sends tingles through your body just thinking about it.

While it's not a subject you want to confront in your initial email exchange or phone conversations because it may give the wrong first impression, it is a part of exploring the possibility of relationship. Most men want to know fairly quickly that a woman doesn't have sexual hang-ups or is sexually inhibited. Most women want to get a feel for what kind of a lover he might be.

It's a good idea to put feelers out and test the waters before you get into a serious relationship. Is he/she as interested in sex as you are? Does he/she feel it's an important part of relationship? What's his/her sexual style — gentle, dominant, kinky? As you get to know each other, little remarks and playful innuendo can reveal a lot and heighten interest.

We all have a deep need to be needed and desired and to live with passion. While it's unlikely that you'll be compatible long term if there is no chemistry, it's sure that if chemistry is all there is, you're doomed to fail. Of course physical chemistry is so important. Without it, eventually one or the other will go looking elsewhere.

If you have good sexual chemistry with your partner it can be 20% of your relationship and provide a great foundation of intimacy that helps deal with the daily challenges of life. If you have bad sexual chemistry with a partner it can be 80% of the relationship and complicate things. If you're looking for long term happy relationship, poor sexual attraction should be a big stop sign. There is value in exploring that chemistry to know if you want the relationship to go any further. However, there is hazard in exploring it too far, too soon.

You don't necessarily want to have sex on your mind from the beginning because it can cloud the important considerations. When physical involvement reaches its peak, it's likely that you'll be reluctant to talk about the things that really matter.

Once you've become physically attached and your perma-smile reveals your carnal bliss, you'll be less likely to want to take the blinders off for fear of finding out something that will shatter the fantasy.

Infatuation is when you think he's as sexy as Robert Redford, as smart as Henry Kissinger, as noble as Ralph Nader, as funny as Woody Allen, and as athletic as Jimmy Conners. Love is when you realize that he's as sexy as Woody Allen, as smart as Jimmy Connors, as funny as Ralph Nader, as athletic as Henry Kissinger and nothing like Robert Redford — but you'll take him anyway.

~ Judith Viorst, (1931-)
American Author, Broadcast
Journalist, Radio host
and Magazine Columnist

Secrets and Cybersex

The internet age is born out of a world of stimulation and instant gratification. Our hyper-speed world bombards with images and adventures, keeps our adrenalin pumping and has us addicted to seeking more. As we've become accustomed to the daily barrage of sexually suggestive multi-media images, it's no wonder that pre-marital and extra-marital sex has become the norm.

Pursuing sex online has become a popular pastime for many men and women. Porn sites and erotica are ever increasing in popularity as people turn to cybersex as a stimulating substitute failing relationships or fill a void without addressing the real problem. The sad reality is that for many, surfing for cybersex becomes a problematic addiction of which they just can't get enough. Surfing sex sites may seem relatively harmless. However, the motivations and the secrecy behind cybersex addictions are so powerful they can create serious problems in happy relationships and in the end destroy families.

You're likely to run into people who turn to the internet for sexual gratification; many are secretly addicted to the thrill of sexy internet chats, many secretly married. In fact, more and more research is coming out to support the theory that the internet is the most significant influence in divorce. The reality is that the internet age has made searching for sex (or a new relationship to replace a spouse) accessible, affordable and convenient with low-risk of being caught.

Making love can be the most uplifting, relationship-deepening, beautiful experiences a couple can share. Making love to the wrong person can be the most heart-breaking, humiliating, and humbling experiences a person can endure.

~ Stephany

Internet Love or Lust?

Lust can seduce you into believing you are compatible with someone when you are really only hot for them. Having great chemistry is important of course. But is it love for the person or lust for passion? Can you see who they really are beyond the physical chemistry of your relationship?

The thing to remember is that lust does not equal love, desire does not equal passion and physical chemistry does not equal compatibility. Desire can grow or fade just as love can, depending on what type of compatibility is fanning the flames. Only passion is sustainable, lust is not.

While physical chemistry stimulates interest and desire, it's not the glue that binds. Physical attraction ebbs and flows, comes and goes and when it's gone even temporarily, it will be common bonds, interests and emotional attachment that keep it together and provide opportunity to restimulate attraction.

Advocating saving the bedroom for later may not be a popular modern point of view. However, most couples find that as they take time to explore each other's common likes, dislikes, values and dreams, their appreciation and attraction grows with excitement.

The more you find in common, the more you want to be together and the more passionate you become.

Take the time to score attraction points in each other's book, let the anticipation build

and you'll both win. Time allows an emotional attachment to grow along with desire, loyalty and respect. Time gives a chance for physical lust to grow into true passion.

Postpone having sex with your new partner for as long as possible, until you are really sure you are compatible, feel their heart and just can't stand it any longer. Every individual has their own moral conscience. This isn't about judgment it's about really getting to know everything you can about this person before you take the most intimate step and risk putting blinders on.

What's Expected and What to Expect

Nothing. No one should expect you to have sex with them and you should not expect it either. It is true even in this modern age that some men treat women as if they are owed something after they have wined and dined and offered gifts. On the other hand some women want to have sex immediately out of a need to prove to themselves that they are desirable and still have it.

TOP 10 GUIDELINES FOR KNOWING WHEN TO EXPLORE SEXUAL CHEMISTRY

1. You're satisfied he/she meets your criteria for what you are looking for.
2. You've had the chance to ask and get satisfactory answers about who they are.
3. You are intellectually intimate and emotionally responsive to each other.
4. You spend much more time talking and getting to know each other than you do making out or being physical.

e-dating Story

Disease doesn't pause for menopause

I'm over 50 and a passionate menopausal woman. I had my tubes tied years ago so pregnancy is not a concern. The one time I wasn't careful, I contracted a nasty little STD that will affect me for the rest of my life. It's embarrassing enough to have to visit the doctor regularly and have genital warts surgically removed every so often, but now I relive the discomfort and embarrassment every time I have to tell a new partner. It's important that women like me (age 40 plus) realize that you can't be too careful. In many ways we are more at risk than young people and the rates of STDs and HIV in boomers and seniors are on the rise because we don't pay enough attention.

5. You like and respect this person and feel they respect your values and feelings.
6. You've done your homework and checked their background out a little.
7. You have discussed birth control and sexually transmitted diseases and both of you have been upfront and open about being sexually active.
8. You both agree to practice safe sex. In today's modern reality, it is also wise to insist on the requisite testing prior to becoming intimate.

9. You've experienced a difficult moment together and you are satisfied that he/she responds well to you in stressful situations.

10. You've asked yourself: Would I want to have a child with this person? The point is, if you would not want to have a child with this person's DNA or characteristics or if they would be unworthy to parent your children...why would you want to sleep with them?

When I mentioned this section of the book to a friend, Sue McGarvie (Canada's foremost sex therapist and author of a book called *Quivering Jello, How to Have Mind-Blowing, Toe-Curling Orgasms!*), she reacted strongly saying, "I think you have to let people feel that sex is good and right, and it's OK to have urges and wild sex from time to time. People want to have fun!" Of course she's right...mind-blowing, toe-curling orgasms are really fun! So here it is: Sex is good, fun, and it's great to be wild from time to time...with the right partner! However:

♥ There is certainly no fun in feeling dumped or avoided or losing interest immediately after you've had sex.

♥ It's not fun to find out after the fact that he/she is sleeping with someone else.

♥ There's no fun in getting a false sense of commitment and believing you have a future only to find out later that your partner did not have a future in mind.

♥ It's not fun to get carried away in reckless abandon and then face the scare of an untimely pregnancy.

♥ It's not fun to face the embarrassment of facing your doctor to discuss the nasty little transmitted disease you picked up while you try not to feel stupid explaining why you chose not practice safe sex or require testing.

♥ It's also not fun when it turns out it's not just a scare but a life-altering or life-ending experience.

The Final Word

DON'T MAKE WAVES, GO WITH THE FLOW

It is said, love finds you when you are least expecting it. Perhaps the key is the word "expecting." After one year of defining what I was looking for and diligently surfing for it everyday, there came a point of frustration where I realized I had put much of my life on hold expecting the right guy to show up.

I remember standing in LA with my feet in the ocean. I discovered that it wasn't the e-dating journey I was objecting to, I was having a blast! I was stressed about my expectations. I literally surrendered my expectation of how and when it would happen, letting the water wash away my frustration. I knew I had done my part, now it was time for the universe to take care of the details. I decided to truly let go of my expectations of the outcome and pursue my destiny knowing that eventually the right person would wash upon my shore. After all, who am I to tell God how to do her work?

How long does it take to find the love of your life? For some, it takes weeks; others, months and maybe years. One thing I am sure of is that you'll definitely have fun and learn a lot about yourself while riding the waves. The internet dating world is a vast ocean universe. If you're clear about who you are and what your purpose is, you set a wave in motion and it eventually comes back to you with the right answer.

> *Everyone wants, needs and deserves to live love and life passionately!*
>
> *There are lots of fish in the sea.*
>
> *You don't have to settle when you can surf for the right one.*
>
> *Many will fail going with the flow, aimless in a sea of possibilities.*
>
> *Others will waste energy chasing the wrong fish and let the good ones get away.*
>
> *Some will waste too much time trolling through smorgasbord of choices that either flounder away or die while caught in the net.*
>
> *Don't get frustrated or give up.*
>
> *There are millions of healthy, happy, hand-some and hearty fish in the internet sea.*

E-dating Experts are happy to help you find them.
We can't wait to hear your heart-melting story.

Enjoy the journey!
Stephany

APPENDIX A

The blame game

THE BLAME GAME

Before reading on, please read the beginning of Secret #1, "Where Did All These Garbage Bags Come From?" To get the maximum benefit from this exercise it is critical that you allow yourself the time and space to go through it step by step without reading ahead.

1. Take a lined piece of paper or your journal and line by line write down all the negative terrible things you hated about your ex-partner beginning with "He" or "She." It doesn't matter how long the list is or how many pages, just consider this an opportunity to let go. For example,
   - "She always manipulated people to get her way rather than just coming right out and asking"
   - "He lied to me and others; I couldn't trust him."

- "She was materialistic; if it wasn't the best, she didn't want it."
- "He was selfish; it always about him and what he wanted."
- "She was a workaholic."

2. Next, go back to the beginning, reviewing each statement line by line, and challenge the statement by asking: Is this really and ultimately always true? While it certainly may be true, our perceptions as to the degree that it is true or whether it is always true are jaded by our emotions and experience. If you're honest, you'll realize that nothing is ever 'absolutely' true. Challenge yourself to think of ways that each statement is false and some examples that prove the opposite.

3. Then, go back to the beginning again and review each statement a third time. This time as you read each statement cross out the "He," "Him," "She" and "Her," and replacing it with "I" and "me."

4. Re-read each statement out loud with the "I" and "me" replaced and feel the truth of it. Rewind into the past to find instances and examples where that statement is true of you.

5. Finally, take a fresh sheet of paper and for each statement rewrite the statement beginning with "I forgive myself and _____ for _____."

Isn't it true that we most dislike in others what we most dislike in ourselves? This simple truth frees us to forgive, heal and create new, more positive patterns in our next relationship.

Appendix B

Commonly used acronyms

COMMONLY USED ACRONYMS FOR EMAIL, CHAT ROOMS AND INSTANT MESSENGER

ADDY — email address
ADN — any day now
AFAIK — as far as I know
AFK — away from keyboard
AISI — as I see it
ASAP — as soon as possible
ATM — at this moment
AYR — awaiting your reply
BBL — be back later
BFN — bye for now
BRB — be right back
BTAICBW — but then again I could be wrong
BTDT — been there done that
BTW — by the way
BYAM — between you and me
C4N — caio for now
CUL — see you later

CWOT — complete waste of time
CYA — see ya
DARFC — ducking and running for cover
DTTAH — don't try this at home
DYK — did you know
ETA — estimated time of arrival
ETD — estimated time of departure
EOD — end of discussion
EZ — easy
F2F — face 2 face
FAQ — frequently asked questions
FAV — favourite
FOCL — fall off chair laughing
FOAF — friend of a friend
FTR — for the record

FUBAR — fouled up beyond any recognition
FWIW — for what it's worth
FYI — for your information
GABI — grin and bear it
GBTW — get back to work
GFC — going for coffee
GL — good luck
GMTA — great minds think alike
G2RM — going to read mail
G2G — got to go
HAND — have a nice day
HTH — hope this helps
HYH — hold your horses
IMHO — in my humble opinion
IMPE — in my previous /personal experience
IOW — in other words
IRL — in real life
JFTR — just for the record
JK — just kidding
JOAMON — jack of all master of none
KISS — keep it simple stupid
L8R — later
LMAO — laugh my ass off
LMBO — laugh my butt off
LOL — laugh out loud
ML — more later
NIML — not in my lifetime
NA — not applicable
NM — no message/nothing much
NRN — no reply necessary
OIC — Oh, I see
OMG — oh my god
OTOH — on the other hand
PDQ — pretty darn quick
PLS — please

PU — that stinks
REHI — hello again
ROTFL — rolling on the floor laughing
RUOK — are you OK?
SN — screen name
SNAFU — situation normal all fouled up
SO — significant other
SWAK — sealed with a kiss
TAFN — that's all for now
THX — thanks
TLA — three letter acronym
TTFN — ta ta for now
TTT — to the top
TTYL — talk to you later
TWIMC — to whom it may concern
UR — you are
URL — web page address
WBS — write back soon
WEG — wicked evil grin
WRT — with regard to
WYSIWYG — what you see is what you get
ZZZ — sleeping

We express gratitude
to the following supportive friends, reviewers and e-dating experts:

Tom Antion, Kelly Arcangeletti, Chris & Janet Attwood,
Suze Baez, Brent Bernie, Terry Brock, John Collinge,
Monique Delisle, Ken Foster, "Wild Bill" Glover, Clyde Gums,
Tom Guzzardo, Debbie Gyapong, Stacey Hall,
Mark Victor Hansen, Bill Harrison, Paul Hartunian,
Diedre Howard, Cynthia Kersey, Sharif Khan,
Sue McGarvie, Peggy Miles, Eileen Moore,
Ron Neal, Paul Nichols, Alfred Pedersen, Craig Peterson,
Ed Rigsby, Elizabeth Rock, Teresa Reeve, Craig Senior,
Jan Stringer, Carol Sutton, Brian & Nina Taylor
and many others who offered encouraging words.

*E-books and services
available from*
e-datingExperts.com

e-dating *Secrets*™ Love Quotes

Be sure you receive your FREE* copy of *e-dating Secrets Love Quotes*

Register for
e-dating *University*
Tele-classes — Live or Audio

Start on a Thursday and have e-dating success by Tuesday! En-

roll in our 3-day, 2-hour interactive telephone seminar series and start e-dating with confidence. You'll get it all, FREE books, products, tools and your own personal e-dating Expert coach. This step-by-step program guides you through all the e-dating *Secrets* and strategies for irresistibly attracting the right person, who to respond to and how to respond.

You'll receive a downloadable *e-dating Secrets*™ *Workbook* packed with tools and checklists to guide you. We keep our classes small so your questions are answered and you get results. Participants also receive a free e-dating Secrets e-book, free personal email coaching for 6 months and a subscription to the e-dating Edge™. What are you waiting for? GET IT ALL and let an expert help you find your perfect love match.

Visit *www.e-datingU.com* to check dates and enroll today.

Send your
e-dating *Expressions*
FREE Musical E-cards

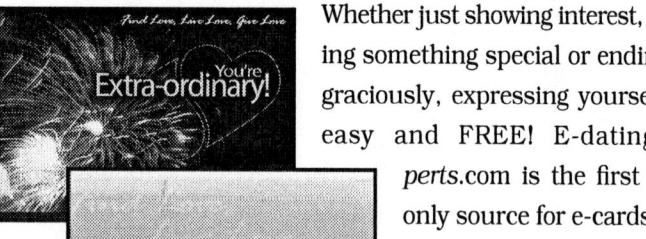

Whether just showing interest, saying something special or ending it graciously, expressing yourself is easy and FREE! E-dating*Experts*.com is the first and only source for e-cards designed specifically to express every stage of the e-dating process. These inspired e-cards are great for any occasion or no occasion at all. They're an excellent way to stay in touch, inspire the heart, and encourage a relationship!

- ♥ Want to save time? Send a quick sentiment along with just the right musical message.
- ♥ Can't find the words? Use one of our heartfelt or humorous quotes cards.
- ♥ Want to send something special? Personalize a card by uploading your own unique photo.

Design your own backgrounds, message text, and brighten someone's day with fun, color and music. We have categories and cards you'll come back to send over and over again.

Check it out at *www.e-datingcards.com*

Get the
e-dating *Edge*™

e-zine FREE... Available NOW!

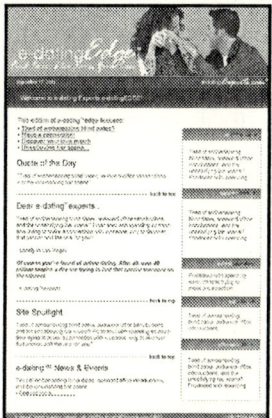

Our FREE *e-dating Edge*™ magazine is your ongoing resource for inspiration and motivation for your online dating journey. You'll get new tips, expert advice, reviews and stories, and special offers delivered by email every couple of weeks. It's like having a personal coach delivered to your inbox. The *e-dating Edge* offers the most current perspectives, unique information and personal coaching. Become an e-dating expert friend and get the edge!

Go to *www.e-datingEdge.com* and subscribe today!

~

CHECK OUT THE OTHER RESOURCES AVAILABLE TO YOU

- ❤ e-dating *Experts* — On-Call Coaching
- ❤ e-dating *Experts* — Book Series and Co-authors
- ❤ e-dating *Experts* — Top 10 Tips Collection
- ❤ e-dating *Experts* — Events & Excursions

e-dating *Secrets* Stories

What's your e-dating story?

Dream Dates and Dating Disasters, Heart-moving Stories of Online Love

We want your heart-melting e-love story, dating disaster or anecdote in our next book. We'll soon be offering prizes and looking for stories that...

- ♥ Put a smile on someone's face
- ♥ Touch the heart or soul of love
- ♥ Change perceptions of e-dating
- ♥ Inspire someone's hope in true love

Our e-dating success stories are written by and about real people with real experiences. They prove it is really possible to make quality connections, live romantic adventures, find your soul mate, and even marry the love of your life through online dating. Of course not every date is perfect, and some provide valuable lessons. So help us share e-dating disaster stories and little anecdotes of experience that help avoid the pitfalls to real love.

Submit your story, dating disaster or anecdote today. If we publish your story in our next book we'll enter you in our prize draws and send you 10 free copies to share with and encourage your friends.

Submit to *stories@e-datingexperts.com* or visit *www.e-datingStories.com*

e-dating ♥ Secrets ™

Printed in the United Kingdom
by Lightning Source UK Ltd.
108449UKS00001B/320